Group's EMERGENCY RESPONSE
HANDBOOK

for: **PARENTS**

Loveland, Colorado
group.com

Group resources really work!

This Group resource incorporates our R.E.A.L. approach to ministry. It reinforces a growing friendship with Jesus, encourages long-term learning, and results in life transformation, because it's

Relational
Learner-to-learner interaction enhances learning and builds Christian friendships.

Experiential
What learners experience through discussion and action sticks with them up to 9 times longer than what they simply hear or read.

Applicable
The aim of Christian education is to equip learners to be both hearers and doers of God's Word.

Learner-based
Learners understand and retain more when the learning process takes into consideration how they learn best.

Group's Emergency Response Handbook for Parents
Copyright © 2009 Group Publishing, Inc.

Visit our website: **group.com**

This book is designed to help you make informed decisions about your child's development and behavior. It is not intended as a substitute for any treatment that may have been prescribed by your doctor. If you suspect that your child has a medical, psychological, or developmental problem, we urge you to seek competent professional help.

Unless otherwise noted, Scripture quotations are taken from the Holy Bible, New Living Translation, copyright © 1996, 2004. Used by permission of Tyndale House Publishers, Inc., Carol Stream, IL 60188. All rights reserved.

Credits
Chief Creative Officer: Joani Schultz
Contributors: Linda Brown, LCSW; Tori Dabasinskas, MFT; Jennifer Diebel; Laura Greiner; Janna Kinner, MSW; Scott M. Kinner; Corrine Knudsen, MSW; Gina Leuthauser; Lisa Lewis; Renee Madison; Denise Payne, MS; Siv M. Ricketts, M. Div.; Jennifer Sifuentes, LCSW; Jennifer Root Wilger
Senior Editor: Candace McMahan
Editor: Jennifer Root Wilger
Copy Editor: Lyndsay Gerwing
Art Director: Jeff A. Storm
Print Production Artist: Pamela Poll
Cover Art Director/Designer: Jeff A. Storm
Production Manager: DeAnne Lear

Library of Congress Cataloging-in-Publication Data
Group's emergency response handbook for parents.
    p. cm.
  ISBN 978-0-7644-3824-0 (pbk. : alk. paper)
 1. Parenting–Religious aspects–Christianity. 2. Parent and
child–Religious aspects–Christianity. 3. Crisis management–Religious
aspects–Christianity. I. Group Publishing. II. Title: Emergency
response handbook for parents.
  BV4529.G77 2009
  248.8'45–dc22
                                2008029275
ISBN: 978-0-7644-3824-0
10 9 8 7 6 5 4 3   18 17 16 15 14 13 12
Printed in the United States of America.

Contents

Introduction

It's tough being a parent, even in the best of times. Besides being mom or dad, you may also get to be coach, chauffeur, nurse, cook, teacher, secretary, counselor…and on and on. Parenthood is overwhelming enough when your children are experiencing smooth sailing in life. Bookstore and library shelves (and maybe even your home) are overflowing with books to guide you through the daily trials of parenting.

But what about the worst of times, the really big storms? You know your preteen daughter is expected to start showing interest in boys soon, but what do you do if she's already having sex? Or considering suicide or harming herself when she experiences rejection? How do you stop your younger child's little white lies from snowballing into an avalanche of deception and distrust?

No matter where you are on your parenting journey, this book can help. It's never too soon or too late to reach out to your hurting child. *Group's Emergency Response Handbook for Parents* will help you learn to listen for your child's cries for help (whether silent, whispered, spoken, or shouted) and respond with competence and compassion.

Of course, it would be great if you never had to pick up this book! But the reality is that every parent faces tough times. So when you see that your child is lonely, rebellious, unmotivated, depressed, or stressed out…pick up this guide. Use the table of contents to find the specific situation you're struggling with, and then flip to that section.

Once there, you'll find a **real-life narrative**—a story from someone who has been there. Sometimes the stories are inspiring, and you'll read how a parent helped a child avert suicide or rebuilt a relationship damaged by rebellion and lies. Other times they're heart-rending and tell stories of families torn apart by divorce or addiction. Either way, these stories will move you and will show you the important difference you can make in the life of your child.

Each section also includes **care and counseling tips**—first steps and next steps you can take to meet the challenge with love and grace. From preschool to preteen and beyond, these ideas will help you effectively support your hurting child.

Next, you'll find **home-life tips**. These practical ideas will encourage you as you work to make your home a safe haven for your child and family in this challenging time. Sometimes little changes can make a big difference, and here you'll find useful tips that will help shift your focus from your child's problem to positive solutions you can implement immediately.

And finally, you'll find an invaluable section on **what to say** and **what not to say** to your child. Proverbs 15:1 says, "A gentle answer deflects anger." This section will help you keep your own emotions in check as you respond lovingly to your child in difficult times.

Each chapter also includes a list of Scripture references to bolster your faith and guide your prayers—for your child and for yourself. And should you encounter a situation that's simply too overwhelming, you'll also find a list of additional resources and recommendations for when to seek help from a professional counselor. In a crisis, this book can guide your first response, but it doesn't take the place of the legal or medical advice you may receive from a professional who knows your child and family.

Many parents, writers, and counselors contributed to this book. Each brings a unique perspective, but through this book, we are all joining you on your parenting journey. God also goes before you. Day or night, God watches over your child and family. We pray that this book will remind you that you're not alone and will guide you as you help your child through a difficult time.

CHAPTER ONE

Suicide
Intervening Before It's Too Late

We lived in a quiet, predictable neighborhood where families seemed to live each day with no major upsets or surprises. That is, until my daughter Jen tried to kill herself.

Jen had always been a quiet girl, and as she grew into a teenager, she became involved in sports and our church youth group. But shortly after Jen turned 15, her easygoing, quiet spirit seemed to take a dip into the gray waters of depression. I noticed, but I couldn't or wouldn't admit that Jen was different. I kept saying that she was just being a "moody teenager." However, when my husband of 20 years, Jen's father, told me he was leaving our family for another woman, things began to get worse—for Jen and for me. Sadly, I did not have an ounce of energy to give to my already descending daughter. My own grief and depression wrapped me in a cocoon of self-pity.

Over the next few months, I watched our family fall apart as if viewing a sad movie from my couch. My oldest daughter escaped to college the summer before Jen's junior year of high school. The overwhelming cost of divorce sent Jen and me to another town in search of a job and affordable housing.

We started settling in and found a new church that seemed to fit us. I began to search for God amid the rubble. Jen didn't want to go to youth group, and at first I respected her wishes. But eventually I began to insist that she go because I was desperate to do something to help her.

Shortly after Jen started at her new school, she announced that she had decided not to try out for soccer because it was "too hard being at a new school." I cringed each day as I sent her off to fight for a place of significance in her shrinking world, but I hardly noticed when Jen began to drift away from me. My heart and mind were full of my own pain as I struggled with the demands of being a single mother.

Jen, who I used to know so well, was suddenly a stranger to me, even though we lived in the same house. Whenever we did talk, Jen brushed me off as if I were a pesky mosquito. My daughter began to spend her weekends and evenings in her room doing who knows what. Most of these changes could be excused as a normal part of adolescence; however, Jen seemed to take the typical teenage separation from parents to an extreme. She didn't even ask to hang out with friends or obsess over what she should wear.

When I saw scabs on Jen's arms late one afternoon, I cautiously asked what caused them. Jen looked at the floor and tapped her feet nervously. She said she had scratched her arms while working on an art project at school and that they didn't hurt. She quickly went to her room for the rest of the afternoon and evening, as had become her routine. An ominous thought that Jen might be in danger floated into my mind, but I pushed it aside as I had done with so many of my fears. I told myself that the scratches had just been an accident and that only severely abused kids did that sort of thing.

Jen began skipping school to sleep in as I went to work early. When the school called to say that Jen was in danger of flunking most of her classes, my former straight-A-and-B student's only excuse was "the teachers at this new school are horrible."

The youth leader called our home one night to say that he was worried about Jen because, though she came to youth group every Sunday, she sat in the back and never said anything. He said she seemed isolated and was easily annoyed with the other kids. I excused her behavior by explaining that the divorce and move had been rough. I assured him that Jen would come out of her funk soon. After I hung up with the youth leader, I considered finding a counselor for Jen. But before I could follow through, I was faced with the darkest and scariest situation imaginable.

The next night I woke up in the middle of the night to get a drink of water (not a normal nocturnal habit for me). As I walked by Jen's room, I saw that her light was on. I knocked softly. No response. With a sense of foreboding, I cautiously crept into the room, but nothing could have prepared me for what I saw.

Jen lay motionless on the floor in the fetal position. My breath left my chest, and I couldn't make my body move for what seemed like hours. As I rushed toward Jen, I saw an open bottle of pain medication on the nightstand. I shook Jen and sobbed, but she didn't respond. As I raced for my cell phone, I thought, "She's gone; my baby's gone." I dialed 911, praying that God would spare my precious daughter's life.

As they loaded Jen into the ambulance, a surprising wave of peace came over me, as if God was telling me that Jen and our family would be OK. In the ambulance, I continued to pray as paramedics pumped my delicate daughter's stomach and worked to get her vital signs functioning normally again.

The next morning, Jen woke up and saw me lying in the hospital chair near her bed. She tearfully confided that she couldn't believe God cared enough about her to keep her alive. I sobbed as I held her in my arms. Through my tears, I gently asked, "Why didn't you tell me how bad things were?"

Jen responded in a shaky voice, "You have too much to worry about, and I thought you would be better off without me."

Just then there was a knock on the door. Jen's youth leader came in. He sat down quietly beside the bed and asked if he could pray for us. He prayed for Jen's healing and that she would find the right people to help her get well. His sweet prayer touched my heart. I silently agreed with his words and asked God to help lead our family out of this pit and into a life of honesty with each other and with him.

Care and Counseling Tips

THE BASICS

As a parent, you're unlikely to face anything that frightens you as much as a child or teen who is considering suicide. You might have noticed that he or she has been withdrawn or depressed recently, but, like Jen's mother, you've probably never thought your child was suicidal.

Depression is a serious mood problem that can feel painful and isolating for the child suffering from it. Depression affects how kids feel and behave in all environments—at school, at home, at church, and even with their friends. Since depression can also be accompanied by other mood or behavior problems, just figuring out how to help may seem overwhelming.

Detecting the presence of suicidal thoughts is an important first step. Some children and teens will tell you directly that they're thinking about suicide. For others, you'll have to know warning signs, which fall into two categories: what the child says and what the child does.

+ What Your Child Says

- Any comment that implies life isn't worth the effort—for instance, "Life's too painful; I don't think I want to deal with it anymore."
- Any comment that shows your child believes there's no solution to his or her problems—for example, "There's no way out of this mess."
- Any statement implying that others would be "better off" if he or she weren't around.
- An offer to give up some essential possessions because he or she won't need them any longer.
- Any indication that your child may take revenge by hurting himself or herself—for instance, "She'll wish she hadn't said that when I'm gone."

+ What Your Child Does

Sometimes a suicide attempt is impulsive, but often it isn't, and the person plans for it. You may notice that your child begins to give away personal items or engage in dangerous activities such as alcohol and drug use. Other signs include dramatic mood changes, intense anxiety, or signs of depression. Most important, if your child has begun to develop a plan, such as buying a weapon, storing up pills, or thinking of a specific scenario such as jumping off a nearby bridge, he or she is at *high* risk of suicide.

FIRST STEPS

When there is an immediate threat of suicide, the first step is to ensure your son or daughter gets professional help.

+ Stay calm.

Take a deep breath and say a silent prayer for protection and comfort for your child.

+ Ask your child directly, "Are you thinking about committing suicide?"

Many parents hesitate to ask this question because they fear it will be offensive or will plant the idea of suicide in a child's mind. This is a myth. By addressing the issue directly, you're more likely to communicate genuine concern and that you understand the seriousness of the situation. This question will also help you determine if your child or teen has a specific plan.

+ Ask, "Do you have a plan?"

Kids who have planned how they would commit suicide are much more likely to follow through than those who haven't. In either case, however, take action by getting professional help.

+ Take the problem seriously and express your concern.

Never doubt that your son or daughter is actually considering suicide. Instead, assure him or her that you will be supportive in this crisis. Listen carefully without judgment or criticism. Though it may be difficult, it's important that you put your emotions aside in order to help.

+ Get help immediately.

Take your child to the local emergency room or mental health center. If your child is not willing to go for help, call the National Suicide Prevention Lifeline (1-800-273-TALK) or 911 (see "When to Seek Help" on page 13).

NEXT STEPS

By now you have helped your child engage in professional help. Now your job is to support the professional services your son or daughter is receiving and encourage healing in the home. Your contributions may include any of the following:

+ Participate in family therapy.

Many mental health professionals agree that individual therapy is effective for depressed and suicidal children but can be enhanced by adding family therapy. Also, mood disorders such as depression sometimes run in families, so your child's therapist may recommend that you seek individual counseling if you are struggling with depression yourself.

Including supportive people such as parents and other family members in treatment serves many purposes: It gives the therapist a clearer and more realistic picture of your child's home life, reinforces for your child the importance of talking about feelings and emotions, and helps you feel more supported in parenting your child through this crisis. Don't forget to include your other children and anyone else who has been affected by your child's situation.

+ Openly talk about suicidal feelings.

Kids need to talk about their feelings with someone besides a counselor. Don't be afraid to ask your child if he or she is continuing to have suicidal thoughts. You won't be planting these thoughts if they aren't already there. Don't let suicidal thoughts be an "elephant in the room" between you and your child. You may feel awkward talking about it at first, but your child will appreciate you bringing it up in a matter-of-fact way.

+ Involve your child in activities.

Get active as a family! Eat dinner together, take walks, plan day trips. Kids who are depressed might not have the motivation to initiate these activities, so be persistent. Try giving two choices, such as "Do you want to go to the mall or to the park?" rather than "What do you want to do?" (Which may get a response such as "nothing" or "I don't know.") Participating in leisure activities with family and friends will help decrease your child's isolation and provide social activities to look forward to.

+ Take care of yourself.

Living with a child who is depressed can be physically, emotionally, and mentally draining. It's OK to take a break and treat yourself to a spa day, night out, or time away with your spouse. Don't shoulder the burden alone; involve others such as your pastor, friends, and extended family members in caring for your child and your family.

WHEN TO SEEK HELP

Consider seeking help from a Christian licensed mental health professional when:

+ Daily functioning is impaired.

If your child or teen is unable to get out of bed, eat, groom, or bathe, get help.

+ Your child is a danger to himself or herself.

If your son or daughter engages in self-injurious behaviors such as cutting, biting, or scratching, get help. (For more information, see Chapter 10, p. 121).

+ Your child is a danger to others.

If your child or teen expresses a desire to harm another person, contact a mental health professional, and notify the person whom he or she has plans to harm.

+ ALWAYS! When a child discloses that he or she is considering suicide or self-harm.

Don't leave your child alone. Together, call the National Suicide Prevention Lifeline (1-800-273-TALK). If your child is unwilling to talk to someone about his or her feelings and plans, you can call 911 for an emergency response team or drive your child to the nearest emergency room.

Home Life

✛ Teach thought-stopping.

Kids who are depressed often make self-deprecating remarks such as "No one likes me," "I'm worthless because I keep messing up," and "I'm not good enough." Your child might also become excessively worried about things beyond his or her control.

Challenge these negative patterns by teaching your child "thought-stopping." Begin by pointing out specific remarks that concern you, and ask if you can tell him or her when you hear these comments in the future. Make a game out of saying "Stop!" and holding up your hand when your child is making negative comments. You'll be helping your child identify the patterns that exist in his or her thinking.

Once older kids can recognize these thoughts, take this idea a step further by putting a poster of a stop sign in his or her room at home or in a school notebook. Having a visual reminder to stop negative thinking will reinforce the new behavior.

✛ Shift your family's focus.

Is your child learning negative thinking patterns at home? With all of the stresses families experience these days, carefully (and prayerfully) consider how much quality time you are spending with your kids and what messages they are learning about themselves in your home. If your family is stressed and stretched too thin, involve everyone in creating some solutions. Sometimes little things like starting a once-a-month Family Fun Day can shift a family's focus and foster more positive interactions.

✛ Establish a routine.

Children and teens with depression often have problems sleeping (too much or too little) and eating (loss of appetite or overeating). Encourage regular bedtimes and healthy eating habits. Although they may resist initially (especially if earlier bedtimes are involved), once they begin to regain energy, most kids will embrace and thrive on a consistent routine.

+ Don't ignore the siblings.

Suicidal threats or attempts naturally shift your attention to your hurting child. But make sure you don't ignore the needs of your other children. Start by carving out five minutes of special time for each child per day, and make sure that you give 100 percent of your attention to that child during that time. By offering each child a time of undivided attention, you can help all of your kids feel heard and understood.

SUICIDE AND THE YOUNG CHILD

While suicide is more common among teenagers, you might have a younger child who suffers from depression or who has experienced trauma. Look for these symptoms that may indicate suicidal thinking in younger kids:

+ **Aggression**—Some children who experience depression act out aggressively—either verbally or physically. The child may target the attack at himself or herself (cutting or scratching, self-deprecating remarks); another person (kicking, hitting, or antagonizing adults or other kids); or objects (slamming doors, punching walls). (See Chapter 10 for a more detailed discussion of self-injurious behaviors.)

+ **Isolation**—Children who are depressed tend to isolate themselves socially. Check with your child's teacher to see if he or she spends a lot of time alone or seems to lack social skills with peers.

+ **Withdrawn**—Dramatic mood changes, including apathetic behavior during activities that used to be fun, can be an indication of depression.

+ **Other Changes**—Pay attention to changes in your child's normal habits, such as eating or sleeping more or less than usual.

What Not to Say

+ "I dare you to do it."

Don't laugh—this happens, and people who say it are usually well-intentioned. People think that they'll call the person's bluff by essentially telling him or her to do it. This is a *bad* idea. In the child's hopeless state of mind, it may be further evidence that he or she isn't valued.

+ "Sure, I promise not to tell anyone."

Don't let yourself be sworn to secrecy. Also, don't worry if you have already agreed to secrecy. Let your child know why you won't be able to keep the agreement. He or she may be upset at first but will thank you in the long run. Feel confident that it's in your child's best interest to speak with others.

+ "Suicide is a sin."

The last thing your hurting child needs is an intellectual or theological debate. Instead, he or she is probably craving someone who will be emotionally present. You can be far more helpful if you work hard to empathize with your child and convince him or her to seek professional help.

+ "You're a depressed kid."

Learn to separate the mood disorder from the child. If you've been living with difficult behaviors for a long time, it might be hard for you to imagine your child without depression. Instead, focus on the positive and point out your child's strengths.

+ "Just think positive."

This statement doesn't take into account your child's feelings and worries. Positive thinking is something to work toward, but it isn't an easy fix. Listen nonjudgmentally and include your child in thinking of a few positive things he or she will be able to focus on.

What to Say

+ "Are you feeling suicidal?"

Don't be afraid to continue checking in on your child's feelings. By being upfront in asking this question, you're opening a door for your son or daughter to trust you if he or she does need help. If not, you won't be planting an idea that isn't there.

+ "What can you do to make this situation better?"

Sometimes the negative statements that kids with depression make (such as "No one will ever like me") can sound like complaining. Constantly listening to complaining is draining—for you and your child. Instead of just ignoring these comments, ask for a positive solution. This will help empower your child to see the situation in a positive light.

+ "The part of your personality I like best is..."

Affirming statements help kids realize they are worthwhile, whether they feel like it or not. Stay away from connecting kids' self-worth to their actions ("You're a good kid because you cleaned your room"). Instead, focus on the God-given traits that make him or her unique ("I really appreciate your helpfulness and generosity"). Watch your child's self-esteem grow!

+ "I love you, and God loves you, too."

This may seem simple, but sometimes kids who struggle with depression lose sight of the fact that people do care! As a parent, your love and acceptance are critical to your child, whether your child realizes it or not. This statement also reminds him or her that God is present and loving.

SCRIPTURE HELP

These Scriptures can help you and your child face thoughts of suicide together.

+ **Psalm 25:4-7, 15-21**
+ **Psalm 77**
+ **Lamentations 3:19-26**
+ **Matthew 11:28-30**
+ **Matthew 26:36-38**

+ **Romans 8:35-39**
+ **2 Corinthians 1:3-11**
+ **Philippians 4:6**
+ **Hebrews 12:12-13**
+ **1 Peter 5:7-10**

IF YOUR CHILD HAS COMMITTED SUICIDE

The death of a child is a tragic personal loss, but it's even harder to understand when the death is caused by suicide. Your family may experience anger toward God, have questions about why your child made that choice, and even turn away from God for a period of time. Your friends and extended family might say insensitive things or not know how to react.

Only time and prayer can truly heal your anger and pain. However, it may be helpful to seek support from parents who have had similar experiences (try www.parentsofsuicide.com or other online communities). Seek guidance and counseling from your pastor or a Christian counselor, and turn toward your spouse during this family crisis rather than allowing your grief to pull you apart.

ADDITIONAL RESOURCES

+ Books

The Power to Prevent Suicide: A Guide for Teens Helping Teens. Richard E. Nelson, Ph.D., and Judith C. Galas. Minneapolis, MN: Free Spirit Publishing, 2006.

When Nothing Matters Anymore: A Survival Guide for Depressed Teens. Bev Cobain, R.N.C. Minneapolis, MN: Free Spirit Publishing, 2007.

Raising a Moody Child: How to Cope with Depression and Bipolar Disorder. Mary A. Fristad, Ph.D., and Jill S. Goldberg Arnold, Ph.D. New York: Guilford Press, 2003.

The Childhood Depression Sourcebook. Jeffrey A. Miller, Ph.D. Los Angeles: Lowell House, 1999.

The Depressed Child: A Parent's Guide for Rescuing Kids. Dr. Douglas A. Riley. Dallas: Taylor Publishing Company, 2001.

Please Don't Label My Child: Break the Doctor-Diagnosis-Drug Cycle and Discover Safe, Effective Choices for Your Child's Emotional Health. Dr. Scott M. Shannon and Emily Heckman. New York: Rodale Books, 2007.

+ Online Resources

www.stopasuicide.org (Screening for Mental Health, Inc.)

www.suicidepreventionlifeline.org (National Suicide Prevention Lifeline)

www.suicidology.org (American Association of Suicidology)

www.medicinenet.com/depression_in_children/article.htm (Medicine Net)

http://health.groups.yahoo.com/group/SMHAI-Parents/ (Suicide and Mental Health Association International)

CHAPTER TWO

Sexual Activity
Protecting and Guiding a Child
Who May Be Sexually Active

These separate interviews are with Morgan, a 17-year-old high school junior who has been sexually active for almost two years, and her parents. Morgan is four months pregnant.

Emergency Response Handbook: *How long had you been having sex before you got pregnant?*

Morgan: I wasn't "having sex." This was the first time. My boyfriend and I were messing around in a room during a party at a friend's house, and we just got carried away. We went back to his house because his parents weren't home and had sex that one time. Until then we had only touched each other and did some oral stuff. But that was it. I never thought it would lead to real sex or me getting pregnant.

ERH: *So when does messing around turn to sex?*

Morgan: I had always thought it wasn't sex until you're naked and having intercourse. Everything else was just different ways to show your love—like kissing, but different ways than just kissing. Now I see that even those things can make you weak when it comes to real sex.

ERH: *Do you think your parents would agree with that?*

Morgan: No—well, I don't know. They would definitely agree that messing around can make you weak against temptations. But I think we disagree on the "when is it sex" thing. My mom and dad are pretty old-fashioned. They never let me close the door to my room when my boyfriend was in there with me.

ERH: *Why not?*

Morgan: They were just trying to protect me. I kept telling them nothing would happen. I guess something did, huh?

ERH: *Did your parents know you were doing these things?*

Morgan: If they did, they didn't ask me about it or talk about it. I think they get all weird when it comes to sex stuff. It's like sex doesn't exist. They would just ignore it; we never talked about it. I just had to learn on my own.

It's been like that since junior high. I had to learn by myself about relationships and sex and stuff—or from friends. And one friend says one thing, like you're not in love until you sleep together. Another friend says something else, like you should wait until after high school and move in together first.

At church we talk about abstinence and how it's important. We talked about contraceptives in one of my classes when I was a freshman, but I didn't know enough about sex to know when you'd need a contraceptive in the first place. It's just a confusing mess of different messages from different people. So I did what I thought felt right…and what I thought other kids my age would have done. Now I kind of wish my parents had talked to me before.

ERH: *Now that you're pregnant, your parents talk to you about it every now and then, right?*

Morgan: Yeah, it took them awhile to open up. But I guess it took me awhile to tell them, too. I felt lonely, and I needed someone to talk to. I was afraid of how they'd react when I told them. I thought they'd say things like "I told you things would get out of hand" or "What were you thinking?"

I didn't want to deal with that kind of response when I found out I was pregnant. I was scared and nervous. Everything was so different. I saw myself differently. I knew my parents would, too.

ERH: *How did they respond?*

Morgan: Just like I expected. I'm kind of glad I waited to tell them, because I wouldn't have been able to deal with it at first.

My mom seemed shocked; then she started crying. She asked me why I'd done something so stupid. My dad got real quiet like he does when he's really mad. He just walked out of the room, and I didn't see him for, like, an hour. Then he came back and said, "I can't believe he did this to you." Then he left again.

The rules in the house quickly changed. I had to come straight home after school; I couldn't keep my job; I wasn't allowed to have Connor over. It was horrible for a while. Then we had a good talk about it, and the rules lightened up a bit.

ERH: *What did you talk about?*

Morgan: I told my parents I was sorry I hurt them, that I didn't mean to hurt them. They listened to me tell them how scared I was and how sorry I was to take it this far. Then they said they were disappointed in the choices I made but that they still love me. It was good to hear that.

After that, my mom took me to the doctor to get checked out. Then we talked to a counselor about options for the baby and me. It was nice to finally have my parents supporting me and talking about my sexual choices. Wow, I never thought I'd say that.

Chris and Katherine are Morgan's parents. Morgan waited two months to tell them she was pregnant.

Emergency Response Handbook: *Did you know Morgan was sexually active before she told you she was pregnant?*

Chris: Not really, no.

Katherine: We knew she was sneaking out and spending a lot of time with Connor. She seemed to be hiding parts of their relationship—a few times we caught them with the door closed kissing a little more passionately than any parent is ready to see. So I guess we had a suspicion, but we didn't really "know."

ERH: *What feelings did you have when she first told you she was pregnant, and how did you express them?*

Katherine: I remember crying immediately. I thought we had really messed up on this one. I blamed myself. Then I felt helpless. I thought that since I've lost my daughter, there was nothing else I could do.

Chris: I was angry. Angry at Connor for laying a hand on my daughter. Angry at Morgan for putting herself in that situation. But most of all, I was angry at myself. I had to get out, so I went and worked in my shop for an hour or so. I didn't know how to reach out to my hurting daughter. I knew she was hurting at the time, but I was so angry I couldn't see what she really needed.

ERH: *When did you learn how to support your daughter? What happened?*

Chris: I don't think it was a matter of "learning how" to support Morgan. Katie and I talked about it. We talked to several of our friends and our pastor. It was really helpful to lean on others and get their feedback. What we heard came from an overwhelming majority: Just be there. They said that Morgan would feel lonely and confused. She gets so many mixed messages; she doesn't know what's right. She just needed us to be there for her and help her.

Katherine: The big one that surprised me was that everyone suggested going with her to doctor's appointments. They said she may be uncomfortable but that she would secretly cherish having her mom there with her. I think she likes it that I go. She doesn't seem embarrassed. Which makes me feel good. I feel like we're doing something right now.

Care and Counseling Tips

THE BASICS

Kids—especially preteens and teenagers—are attempting to discover who they are, what their role is in society, and what it means to be female or male. As they develop their social identity, they are often confronted with questions concerning their gender identity (their sense of being male or female); their gender role (the behaviors, attitudes, and characteristics associated with each gender); and their sexual choices. Many factors influence this development:

+ Media influence

Our kids are bombarded with inappropriate and unrealistic media images of "ideal" appearance and behavior—from movies, TV, magazines, and commercials. The role models that many kids identify with are often overly sexualized and illustrate extreme sex-role stereotypes: Males are macho and muscular; females are a paradox, both seductive and sexually submissive.

Society doesn't help us as we work to guide our children and teens toward sexual purity. Abstinence is viewed as an archaic idea. In some settings, kids are handed free condoms and told that they are incapable of controlling their urges. Many young people today are rapidly catapulted into an adult world for which they are emotionally unprepared.

+ Adult models

Kids observe the significant men and women in their lives and develop ideas about appropriate ways for each gender to behave. Families tend to have rules surrounding gender roles—some are spoken, and some are unspoken but understood. Your child is observing the roles in your family and starting to integrate that information into his or her identity.

+ Changing bodies

All kids experience curiosity about their bodies, regardless of their stage of development. But adolescence is a period of major growth and change—

physically, emotionally, and cognitively. Since this change happens at a different rate for everyone, your child may feel overwhelmed, confused, and self-conscious about his or her appearance.

+ Fitting in with peers

Preteens and teenagers are also working on figuring out how they fit into the world around them. They're asking questions such as "Who am I?" "Who do I want to be?" "Do I have what it takes to become that kind of person?" They're beginning to make more of their own decisions, such as which friends to spend time with or which activities to be involved in.

Some teenagers and preteens are beginning to be involved in intimate relationships, which can be emotionally confusing, even to adults. It's a major challenge for young people, these not-quite-adults, to navigate the turbulent waters of dating relationships. The sting of rejection and the ache of being unwanted are felt deeply in a teenager's fragile heart.

With all of these influences affecting your child, you may feel that your parental counsel about sexual choices falls on deaf ears. Don't give up! Your message is important, and it can get through. In this chapter, you'll discover how to start communicating now about your child's sexual choices and what you should do if you discover that your child is already sexually active or facing an unplanned pregnancy. With some open communication, patience, and prayer, you can help your son or daughter develop healthy, God-honoring relationships.

FIRST STEPS

If you suspect that your child is sexually active, here are some steps you should take immediately.

+ Stay calm.

Take a deep breath and say a silent prayer for patience and understanding.

+ Listen first.

You will need to confront your son or daughter in a calm, understanding manner. Briefly and factually state your concerns; then be prepared to sit back and listen to his or her side of the story.

✛ Be specific.

Ask, "What is sex?" Your child may define sex differently from the way you do. Sexual behaviors range from holding hands to kissing to oral sex to intercourse. Ask your child to describe the type of sexual behavior that he or she has engaged in.

✛ Be understanding.

Even though you are probably feeling hurt, angry, and frustrated, this is not the time to work out those issues with your child. Thank your son or daughter for being honest with you, and commit to being supportive even though you disagree with his or her choices.

✛ Hold both partners responsible.

Whether male or female, in a consensual sexual encounter, your child is 100 percent responsible for his or her own actions.

✛ Schedule a medical appointment.

If your son or daughter has engaged in oral sex or intercourse, you should schedule an appointment to test for sexually transmitted diseases—regardless of your child's gender and even if you believe this was the first sexual experience for both partners. Girls should also be tested for pregnancy. It's important for your child to understand that there are responsibilities, such as annual pelvic exams, that come along with the choice to be sexually active.

✛ Consider your child's legal situation.

Each state has different laws about the age that a child can consent to sexual activity and the legal age differences between the partners. Contact your local law enforcement or social services department to find out more about your state's laws.

NEXT STEPS

✛ Communicate, communicate, communicate.

When we encounter something new, we often become very curious. Your child will naturally be curious about new things, including sex. Kids and

WHEN TO SEEK HELP

Consider seeking help from a Christian licensed mental health professional if your child is:

+ Living a "double life."
+ Facing an unplanned pregnancy.
+ Struggling with sexual identity or sexual preference issues.
+ Involved in promiscuous sexual activity and putting himself or herself in high-risk situations.
+ Reporting sexual abuse or assault.
+ Feeling significantly distressed about his or her gender identity, appropriate gender role, or sexual choices.

adolescents need to figure out what to do with this new aspect of their lives. Take advantage of this curiosity to open a conversation about sexuality even with your younger children. The best time to talk to your children about sexual choices is long before you discover they are already sexually active. When they have the opportunity to explore, discuss, and learn about their sexuality in safe ways, they will be better equipped to honor God in their sexual decisions.

+ Change your approach.

Preaching to your son or daughter about abstinence isn't enough. Ask tough questions such as "What would your life be like if you became a teen parent?" and "What would happen if you contracted an STD that doesn't have a cure?" Challenge your child to connect his or her current choices to future consequences.

+ Talk about safe sex.

There's a great debate about whether parents should discuss the issue of protection and contraceptives. On one hand, parents feel that talking about it would be condoning the behavior. On the other hand, if your child has made the decision to be sexually active, talking about contraception can help him or her stay safe. If you choose to talk to your child about this sensitive subject, help your child know the reliability of each form of protection or contraceptive and encourage your child to be open and honest with you about how and when protection is used.

+ Be informed.

Your child is bombarded with different media messages about gender identity and sex. How will you know how to challenge these messages if you don't know what they are? Read some teen magazines or watch TV with your son or daughter, and ask open-ended questions about the content. Engaging in a dialogue about what your child sees will give you a chance to share your values.

Wondering what messages your child is hearing in the media? Seventeen magazine recently conducted a survey among American teenagers about their views of sex. When asked, "What makes you NOT a virgin?"
- 15% responded "getting fingered or giving a hand job"
- 29% believe oral sex
- 60% thought it was anal sex
- 76% said a penis entering a vagina, even a little
- 99% responded intercourse that leads to ejaculation

Home Life

+ Begin a dialogue when your child is young.

Start talking about sexual choices early in your child's life. Kids are going to hear about sexual choices somewhere, and it may as well be within the context of a Christian community. Also, talk to your children about their role models and the messages they're getting from the media.

+ Find a balance between independence and supervision.

While teenagers need to experience an increasing amount of freedom and independence, they also need to know that you care enough to check up on them. Make sure your child knows that you will check MySpace or Facebook pages, the texting history on his or her cell phone, and friends' houses or jobs to make sure you know where he or she is. Place your computer in a high-traffic area of your home, and consider using parental controls to monitor TV viewing. If your teenager will be home alone at night, have a friend or neighbor check in frequently.

+ Don't give up or change your expectations and standards.

Keep sexual purity a top priority. Support your child as he or she upholds sexual purity standards, even—or especially—if it seems that no one else is sexually pure. Surround yourself with other Christian parents who can encourage you as you raise a pure teenager.

DATE RAPE

Most sexual assaults are committed by someone known to the victim, so they often go unreported because of the shame, embarrassment, and self-blame that victims frequently experience.

It's important that you teach your son or daughter how to keep himself or herself safe to prevent a sexual assault. Because many rapes are connected with drug or alcohol use, encourage your child to avoid situations in which they or others are using these substances. (If you're concerned that your child might be using these substances, see Chapter 5, p. 60.) Make it clear that you'll gladly pick your child up in situations in which he or she doesn't feel safe. Tell your child that you'll appreciate that he or she called you and that you will withhold judgment. Teach your child to say "no" to unwanted advances. You may even consider taking a self-defense class together.

If you discover that your child has been sexually assaulted or raped, follow these steps:

+ Listen, believe, and accept. It's important for victims to know that someone believes their story.

+ Place the blame where it belongs. Survivors often blame themselves for their trauma. Even if your child placed himself or herself in an unsafe situation or was using drugs or alcohol, the sexual assault was not your child's fault.

+ Encourage action. If the assault has just occurred, discourage your child from cleaning up, showering, or changing clothes, so that the necessary legal evidence can be gathered. Call the National Rape Crisis Hotline (1-800-656-HOPE), and request a trained advocate to walk through the legal and medical procedures and explain the available choices. If the assault occurred in the past, you can still talk to a crisis counselor about your child's options.

What Not to Say

+ "Was it good?"

Don't joke around when someone tells you about sexual choices. Your child will experience enough of this from peers.

+ "You're a slut."

One mother, upon learning that her daughter was sexually active, called her "Jezebel" and the "whore of Satan." Name-calling is never appropriate and may further damage your child's already fragile self-esteem. It will definitely damage your relationship.

+ "Well, you know what the Bible says about purity..."

Sure, the Bible says a lot about sexual purity and choices. However, pointing this out is probably not the first thing you should do. Your child may be struggling with shame and may fear your initial reaction will be judgment. Build trust by listening first. Once you have a better understanding of your child's situation, you may be able to identify Scriptures that will encourage as well as convict your child.

+ "What is your [family member your child looks up to] going to say?"

Finding out that your son or daughter is sexually active might embarrass you, especially if others find out. But you don't need to drag the entire extended family into the situation.

What to Say

+ "If you're mature enough to have sex, you're mature enough to talk about it and consider the consequences."

Part of becoming sexually active means participating in annual physicals

31

and pelvic exams, learning about contraceptives and STDs, and having honest talks with you. If your child chooses to participate in an adult activity like sex, hold him or her accountable for these responsibilities.

+ "The choices you're making are unhealthy."

Don't forget to explain the physical and emotional ramifications of your child's sexual choices. Preteens and teens tend to act impulsively—they probably haven't taken the time to think about how their choices might affect their future.

+ "You are God's child."

Everyone needs to be reminded of his or her identity and value in Christ. God didn't give us sexual mandates because he's a spoilsport. God gave us boundaries to protect our hearts—and our bodies.

+ "What will you do differently next time?"

Kids must have sexual standards in order to make wise choices. Standards may include "I will keep all my clothes on all the time" or "I will not be in my room or a car alone with my boyfriend [or girlfriend]."

+ "God made you in his image."

In the Christian faith, people's bodies are valuable. So much so, in fact, that Christians believe in the resurrection of the body. Teach the significance of the body and how we should use it.

MASTURBATION

Children and teens grow more and more curious about their bodies as they mature. They need to figure out healthy ways to deal with their new discoveries. Body exploration is a natural part of growing up.

It's normal (and common) for young children to touch themselves and masturbate. They're exploring their bodies, not fantasizing about sex. So don't panic. Instead, make sure your young child knows what is private and what is healthy. As your child matures, discuss what a healthy sexual relationship looks like.

As children grow into adolescents, increased curiosity will follow. You may suspect (or even walk in on the act of) masturbation. Even at this age, this is a normal response to hormones and curiosity. Being quick to condemn will do more harm than the masturbation itself. Instead, watch for signs of negative sexual behaviors, like pornography or unsafe sex, and respond to those.

In either case, it's best not to react with anger, shame, or surprise. When kids have the opportunity to explore their sexuality in safe ways, they will be better equipped to honor God in their sexual decisions.

SCRIPTURE HELP

+ **Genesis 2:18-25**
+ **Deuteronomy 26:16-19**
+ **Psalm 32:1-7**
+ **Psalm 46**
+ **John 8:1-11**

+ **1 Corinthians 6:12-20**
+ **Ephesians 2:1-10**
+ **Colossians 3:1-17**
+ **1 Thessalonians 4:1-12**
+ **1 Peter 1:13-25**

ADDITIONAL RESOURCES

+ Books

Someone Like Me: A Youth Devotional on Identity. Annette LaPlaca. Colorado Springs, CO: WaterBrook Press, 2001.

So What Does God Have to Do With Who I Am? Joey O'Connor. Grand Rapids, MI: Revell Books, 2001.

Passport to Purity. Dennis and Barbara Rainey. Little Rock, AR: FamilyLife Publishing, 1999.

Equipped to Serve: Caring for Women in Crisis Pregnancies, Fourth Edition. Cynthia R. Philkill and Suzanne Walsh. Grand Rapids, MI: Frontlines Publishing, 2001.

A Season to Heal. Luci Freed and Penny Yvonne Salazar. Nashville, TN: Cumberland House Publishing, 1996.

+ Online Resources

www.care-net.org (Care Net)
www.optionline.org
www.freetobeme.com (New Direction for Life Ministries, Inc.)

CHAPTER THREE

Lying
Helping Your Child Limit Lying

"**B**ut, Mom, I'm the honest one!"

Unfortunately, it was true: Jayden *was* the honest child. When Tiffany needed to know what *really* happened, she would pull Jayden aside. Often with tears, but always with sincerity, Jayden would relate the facts. Jayden seemed incapable of persisting in a lie.

"Kelsey shoved me into my dresser!" Jayden gasped, breathing through the tears.

"I did not! Jayden screamed at me to get out of her room, when all I wanted to do was borrow her brush. She fell back when I got the brush off the dresser!"

Kelsey was a different story. Lies spilled from Jayden's older sister's mouth like punch at a preschool birthday party. Tiffany didn't need any more information. The tussle upstairs, the knot on Jayden's head, and the suspicious excuse Kelsey gave pointed to yet another lie.

"Why would you do that, Kelsey? Go to your room right now while I figure out what to do."

"But, Mom!"

"Go, Kelsey!"

Kelsey always had a wild imagination. When she was little, she loved to pretend that the backyard slide was her castle. She would often tell Tiffany of her adventures riding horses, meeting new friends, and dancing at the ball. Kelsey was so sincere that she almost seemed to believe that it had all really happened.

The problem really began once Kelsey started preschool. Kelsey just seemed to be a little more devious—to have a knack for trouble. Kelsey's little lies were so ridiculous; Tiffany often had to hold back laughter.

"Did you take my files off the desk?"

"No, Mommy."

"Well then how did you know the red folder was under Jayden's crib?"

"I had a dream last night that Jayden put it there."

"Wow. That's some dream."

"Want to know what else I dreamed?"

Kelsey was a sharp girl, and Tiffany enjoyed her quick wit and imagination. But as Kelsey progressed through grade school, her little lies started to cause real problems. Kelsey began to lie about getting her homework done. When the teacher collected homework, Kelsey would lie and say that she had forgotten it at home. It seemed that the real problem was that Kelsey was just getting lazy.

Tiffany did her best to confront Kelsey's behavior. But when confronted, Kelsey would blow up and complain that Jayden was "a perfect little baby who is spoiled to death." As a matter of course, Tiffany found that she was constantly asking Kelsey for the truth and doubting most of her responses. Tiffany was growing tired, and Kelsey seemed to be growing more angry and defensive.

At her wits' end, Tiffany asked Kelsey's youth pastor for help. The youth pastor loaded Tiffany up with a stack of parenting books and helps. Tiffany found some strategies and good thoughts in the parenting books. But the real help came from a small pearl of wisdom the youth pastor shared: "If you believe Kelsey is a liar, she won't fall short of your expectations."

The honest truth was that Tiffany really expected Kelsey to lie—the whole family expected it. And Kelsey had come to believe that she was the liar in the family.

The change was slow and almost imperceptible at first. But Tiffany was determined to change her beliefs about her daughter's character and to cease any behavior that reinforced her previous attitude. Tiffany started making small adjustments. Rather than drilling Kelsey on whether she had completed her homework, she would simply ask Kelsey to show it to her. Without the interrogations, Tiffany's interactions with Kelsey began to improve.

The real improvement came when Tiffany intentionally changed the way she related to Kelsey. Tiffany worked to spend time alone with Kelsey in the activities Kelsey enjoyed, such as going to the mall. During those times, Tiffany looked for every opportunity to point out the good she saw in Kelsey. She praised Kelsey for her creativity and reminded her that she was a good and honest person.

Tiffany asked Kelsey about her dreams and aspirations. During one critical conversation, Tiffany asked Kelsey, "What kind of adult do you want to be?" Kelsey responded that she wanted to be an actress and that she wanted to be kind and honest. Tiffany affirmed that potential in Kelsey. Tiffany and Kelsey often return to that conversation when trust issues arise in their relationship.

Kelsey's life is not deception-free. She still sometimes hesitates to bring the full truth forward. She still argues with Jayden, and they both accuse each other when there's a blowup. But Kelsey is no longer seen as the liar of the family. While Kelsey's relationship with Tiffany isn't perfect, there is greater mutual respect and trust between mother and daughter than they've experienced in the past.

Care and Counseling Tips

THE BASICS

It's not a matter of *if* your children will lie to you; it's simply a matter of *when*. During the preschool years, most young children innocently try lying as a part of their rapidly expanding communication repertoire. Young children often aren't completely cognizant of the line between playful imagination and lying about their experiences. As parents, we want to encourage imagination and creativity, so we play along and may even feed the fantasies that serve to help a child elevate his or her self-perception.

Lying to avoid negative consequences soon follows. You may be shocked when your truthful and imaginative child chooses to offer a baldfaced lie in an attempt to divert and avoid parental displeasure. The fact that your child has chosen to lie shouldn't cause consternation. However, many parents struggle to understand and implement a correct response to a lying child. How do you respond when you know your child is lying but you don't have proof? If your child finally tells the truth, should you remove the consequence to encourage future honesty? And how do you answer the inner voice that whispers, "If she lies like this now, what will she be like when she's 15?"

Research shows that children are perfectly capable of lying to their parents while looking them directly in the eye. And as they grow older, they grow more proficient and convincing in this skill. By the teen years, there is no longer anything cute about lying. Teens will naturally explore lying as a method to navigate their way through unpleasant situations. But chronic and recurring deception is usually a symptom that may be covering a deeper problem. If your teen consistently lies to you, he or she is likely involved in some sort of behavior that you would disapprove of and that may prove harmful to him or her. At this stage of development, children have the terrifying ability to lie their way into and around behavior that can have a detrimental impact on the rest of their lives. The information in this chapter will help you identify the causes of deceptive behavior and affirm and support honesty in your family relationships.

FIRST STEPS

Remember that your child's lie is not an indication of direct disrespect or an attempt to devalue your relationship. Rather, your young child is attempting to discover if lying is a useful tool for navigating difficult circumstances. As you work to demonstrate the value of honesty to your child, try to avoid the two extreme responses of either overreacting or ignoring the behavior. Calmly work through the following steps with your child:

+ Practice telling the truth together.

If your child is clearly lying, help your child tell the truth about the situation. Showing young children the illogical aspects of their story or "catching them" in the lie is not as effective as helping them simply relate the truth. You may need to model exactly what your child needs to say. For example, you could say, "Instead of what you just told me, please tell the truth. Try saying, 'I tore up the papers on the desk, Mom.'"

Older children may find this simple approach somewhat insulting. But the basic principle still applies. Rather than playing psychological games or trying to trick your child into admitting the truth, give your child a direct opportunity to explain. If your child holds back or clings to the deception, simply reveal the truth and then ask him or her to explain it. For example, if your child lied about going to a friend's house after school, say, "I know you weren't at Jake's house. Please tell me where you were."

+ Lead your child in making amends.

Regardless of how the truth comes out, require your child to make fair amends for his or her behavior. For example, if your child accidentally crashed his or her bike into your neighbor's car, he or she should tell your neighbor what happened (probably with your oversight) and work out a way to pay back your neighbor. This sort of repentance and honesty in action empowers your child to restore rather than avoid the relationship with the offended person. Making amends can actually turn an embarrassing and shameful event into an empowering situation that builds self-esteem.

+ Reward honesty.

An honest admission of wrongdoing shouldn't necessarily remove consequences or punishment. However, your child should learn from you over time that immediate and complete honesty will lead to less severe consequences than wrongdoing coupled with deception.

NEXT STEPS

Older children and teenagers often use lying as a means of taking the path of least resistance in uncomfortable situations. They may also lie as a reaction to fear, a means of avoidance, or as a response to perceived no-win situations. Navigating deception with older children is a little more complex than dealing with preschoolers, but you have the skills and insight to communicate the value of honesty to your teenager by taking the following common-sense approaches:

+ Help your teenager make the connection between honesty and rights or privileges.

As your teenager proves to be trustworthy, he or she should be given additional freedoms and privileges that correspond with your trust level and are appropriate for his or her age. When your child breaks trust through deception, privileges and freedoms should be restricted until trust is earned again. Clearly explain this process to your teenager so he or she can enjoy the full benefit and accomplishment that comes with earning and keeping your trust.

+ Respond to all lies—even the little ones.

It's tempting to overlook the little and inconsequential fibs that you find your child telling. However, small lies may indicate an iceberg of deception that is hidden from your view. Small lies may also initiate a pattern of behavior that can soon grow out of control for your child. Over time, this consistency will teach your child that confessing the truth always leads to more positive outcomes than getting caught in a lie.

+ Keep focused on the issue at hand.

Sometimes older kids and teenagers may try to dodge the issue of lying by downplaying the significance of the situation. Your child may argue that he or she is basically a good kid and that there are other problems (such as drugs, violence, or sexual activity) much worse than lying. Keep focused, and remind your child that this conversation is not about your insistence on smothering his or her self-expression, freedom, or growth. It's about the fact that your child lied to you. Lying breaks trust, harms relationships, and usually accompanies other negative behaviors.

BUILDING TRUST

There is no substitute for quality time and honest communication when it comes to reducing the probability of deviant behavior in our children.

While not impossible, it is more difficult to lie to people we know, love, and respect. In addition to quality time with your kids, help build a loving and trusting relationship with your child by:

✦ Working hard to have fun with your child through quality time.

✦ Showing consistency in the way you respond to negative behavior.

✦ Setting and enforcing boundaries for your child.

✦ Avoiding emotional and heated battles with your child. Rather, respond calmly, gently, and firmly.

✦ Apologizing when you make a mistake.

✦ Avoiding relating to your child as a peer.

✦ Showing an interest in the things that interest your child.

✦ Making yourself available to listen to your child's needs, concerns, and dreams.

✦ Empowering your child by giving him or her new responsibilities that will help prepare him or her for the next stage of life.

Home Life

✦ Model honesty.

"What you do speaks so loud I cannot hear what you say."

Ralph Waldo Emerson's simple quote speaks volumes to parents trying to model honesty to their children. Your efforts to instill honesty in your child will fail if you aren't modeling honesty. Many of us have even instructed our children to lie:

"Dad, Mr. Williams is on the phone."

"Tell him I'm not here, and take a message."

Think twice before telling a "white lie" or sending the message that an "inconsequential" lie is permissible. For example, if you're in the restroom when the phone rings, just have your child explain that you're unable to come to the phone rather than asking him or her to lie. Patterns of deception begin with small and seemingly inconsequential violations of trust.

✦ Use a trust deposit box.

Use this illustration to help your preschool or early-elementary child understand the effects of broken trust. Set a number of coins in an open shoe box or bowl. Explain that the coins in the box represent the trust you have in your child. Affirm that your child is an honest person and that you have a lot of trust in him or her. Since your trust box is full, you are happy to let your child go over to a friend's house to play, use the Internet, or enjoy other privileges that require trust.

Remove a coin from the box as you relate that when your child lies to you, he or she makes a trust withdrawal or takes away some of the trust you have in him or her. With less trust in the box, it's more difficult for you to allow your child to enjoy privileges. Add a few coins to the box as you explain that when your child confesses the truth—even when he or she likely wouldn't get caught—it adds to your trust. The more trust deposits your child makes, the easier it is for you to allow him or her to enjoy privileges. Check that your child understands by asking him or her to explain how the trust box works.

+ Avoid no-win situations.

Children don't always understand the reasons for rules and may at times protest limits and guidelines that are reasonable, fair, and necessary. But unrealistic or overbearing demands and expectations put enormous pressure on a child. Particularly if your parenting style is more authoritarian, your child may use deception to try to avoid invoking your displeasure. If you believe that you and your child may be in this situation, don't excuse or ignore the lie, but be willing to admit the part you had in creating the circumstances that led to the deception. Talk honestly with your child about the pressure he or she feels; then work to extend grace and a little breathing room.

+ Remember the source.

Scripture says that Satan is the "father of lies" (John 8:44). Jesus, on the other hand, describes himself as "*the* truth" (John 14:6). Teach your children that lies are the source of enormous heartache, including the condition of sinfulness that we all experience. As you build a foundation for honesty in your home, help your children understand that lying leads us to hide from God and others who love us, causes destruction, and damages relationships—just as it did when Adam and Eve heard the first lie.

SCRIPTURE HELP

+ **Exodus 20:16**
+ **Proverbs 6:16-17**
+ **Proverbs 12:22**
+ **Proverbs 19:5**
+ **Proverbs 21:6**
+ **John 8:44**
+ **2 Thessalonians 2:9-10**
+ **3 John 1:4**

What Not to Say

+ "You're such a liar."

If your child believes she is a liar, she will act accordingly. Avoid blanket statements that negatively label your child. Rather, regularly remind your child that you trust him or her and that he or she is an honest person. Your child lied, but your child is *not* a liar. You can reinforce your child's identity as an honest person even in the midst of working through deception. As you confront the lie, you can express a level of surprise or confusion by acknowledging that it is not typical for your child to lie.

+"Why did you lie?"

The answer to this question is usually pretty obvious. Your child lied to avoid negative consequences, avoid discomfort or negative circumstances, or to feel or appear better than he or she is. Your child may or may not be in touch with the needs or issues behind a lie. Asking your child to justify his or her actions forces your child to either soften the facts and intent or to lay bare the depth of darkness in his or her heart. If you suspect there is more negative behavior hidden behind or associated with the lie, ask your child about it directly.

+ "God hates a lying tongue."

While this statement is true (see Proverbs 6:16-17), your child may not be able to process the context of this passage without your help. It's good and important to share God's position on lying. When you do, make certain your child understands that God loves him or her—no matter what. God hates lying because of what it does to the person who is lying and those he or she lies to. Train your child to respect and honor God's holiness, but work hard to help him or her understand that God's love is truly unconditional.

What to Say

+ "Thank you for telling me."

When our children confess shortcomings, slip-ups, or foolish choices, our first reaction is often anger or strong disappointment. Your child's confession of the truth should not necessarily preclude punishment or consequences. However, if your child learns to expect a strong negative emotional reaction when he or she tells you the truth, he or she may start lying to avoid this reaction. You may need to be firm, but always be gentle and *always* listen before you respond.

+ "This could have turned out much worse if you hadn't told the truth."

Even if you catch your child in the lie or have to coax him or her to tell the truth, help your child think about what could have happened if he or she had persisted in the lie. Talk together about worst-case scenarios surrounding the deception to help your child understand where lying can lead. Emphasize how persisting in the lie would force your child to tell more lies, increase the severity of the consequences, and further disrupt trust. As you discuss solutions to make amends for the situation, make it clear that the sooner the truth comes out in any situation, the better.

+ "What could you have done differently to avoid lying?"

Your child may turn to lying to help navigate complex social situations. For example, a good friend may ask your child not to tell others about something he or she has done. In order to protect his or her commitment and preserve the relationship with the friend, your child may lie to you or another person in authority. By talking with your child about how he or she could have handled the situation differently, you can give him or her tools to face similar situations in the future.

+ "Withholding the truth is often just as wrong as lying."

To avoid the punishment that comes with lying or to avoid violating his or her own moral code, your child may simply withhold important details without blatantly lying to you. Help your child understand that both withholding information and lying are tactics we use to hide the truth. If your child doesn't share essential details of the truth, respond the same way you would to lying. Remind your child that you are looking for the truth and expecting him or her not to hide it from you in any way.

ADDITIONAL RESOURCES

+ Books

How to Discipline Your Six to Twelve Year Old...Without Losing Your Mind. Dr. Jerry L. Wyckoff and Barbara C. Unell. New York: Doubleday, 1991.

Boundaries with Teens: When to Say Yes, How to Say No. John Townsend. Grand Rapids, MI: Zondervan, 2006.

Shepherding a Child's Heart. Tedd Trip. Wapwallopen, PA: Shepherd Press, 1995.

WHEN TO SEEK HELP

Chronic lying is often associated with other risky behaviors that can pose a real threat to the safety of your child or others. The following signs may indicate that your child is struggling with deeper issues that lead to recurring dishonesty:

✦ Friends and family members often comment on your child's habit of stretching the truth.

✦ Teachers or other professionals who work with your child bring the problem of lying to your attention.

✦ You have little trust in your child despite your attempts to work through these issues.

✦ You have found other signs of deviant behavior such as drug paraphernalia or merchandise your child cannot afford.

✦ Your child has completely cut off himself or herself from a relationship with you.

Research shows that chronic lying can be a sign of abuse, by which children are attempting to assert control or regain a sense of power. While chronic lying is not always rooted in abuse, it is almost always rooted in a deeper issue that can require professional help.

If you're not certain whether it's time to see a counselor, you can gain insight and perspective from the following:

✦ Talk with another Christian couple you respect who have children older than yours. Describe your situation, and ask if they feel the problems you've seen in your child are a natural part of development or a more serious problem.

✦ Ask your children's pastor for resources and strategies for dealing with dishonesty.

✦ Ask your child's classroom teacher to help support your efforts at home as he or she interacts with your child at school each day.

CHAPTER FOUR

Rebellion
Helping Your Rebellious Child

Raye had a good family, with two parents who loved her and two younger sisters who adored her to the point of annoying her. They attended church together regularly, and each of them also had other ways of being involved: Bible studies, youth group, service activities, and choir. On the surface they looked like an average American family—whatever passes for average these days.

Friends described Raye as quiet. Her parents said she had always been shy and somewhat serious. And she was smart. She was the type who didn't have to study much to get the best grades in school. That would have driven her friends crazy, except that Raye helped them get better grades, so they didn't give her too much grief.

One Friday night Raye went to a slumber party. When her dad came to pick her up in the morning, he discovered she had dyed the tips of her long blonde hair shocking purple. Her dad nearly passed out on the spot. Not wanting to cause a scene, he waited until they got in the car and down the street to let loose. He threatened to drive straight to the salon to have the purple cut off, until Raye reminded him that she needed to be at choir practice.

Raye loved choir. You wouldn't know it by watching her sing, though. She stood stock still, without a smile—indeed, with very little expression. Some of the more joyful praise songs looked a little off coming out of her mouth, because she didn't look joyful. But Raye and the choir director had a great relationship, and she assured Raye's parents that Raye was in the right place.

Raye's dad walked with her into choir practice that morning. He wanted to see the director's reaction just in case he did need to drive her to the salon, or home. Instead, the choir director greeted Raye with a big hug. She offered a surprised smile as she stroked Raye's hair. She didn't exactly say she liked Raye's new look, but she didn't condemn it, either.

So Raye's dad let it go. Raye's mom had to take more than a few deep breaths, but no one made a salon appointment for her. Later that week the choir director related a conversation she'd had with Raye when Raye had dropped by to help file sheet music:

She said she'd be willing to wear her hair pulled back so the congregation wouldn't see the purple while we sing. She knows it upsets you and that it could upset some of the other members. She wants to be respectful, but she also wants to be herself. I know, I know, but that's what she's trying to figure out: Who is herself? *You know, if this is as bad as her rebellion gets, you're pretty lucky.*

In fact, Raye's parents had talked with their friends—in Bible study, in prayer meetings, on the phone—and they heard repeatedly how lucky they were. A smart, serious girl like Raye could blow up. Others had seen it happen. Everyone knew someone who knew someone whose child had rebelled in big ways: skipping or failing school, shoplifting, using alcohol and drugs, having sex, running away. No, they weren't lucky; they were blessed. Purple hair might irritate them, but it was a little thing compared to the alternatives.

Eventually there were other things, too. Sometimes Raye talked back, seemingly for no reason at all. Sometimes she flat-out refused to do home-work or settled for grades that were no more than adequate (unusual for her). One time she went home with an older friend after school without calling. She came home two hours later, went straight to her room, and finished her homework as if nothing out of the ordinary had happened.

But having learned from the purple hair, which after a few months grew out and got cut off, Raye's parents did their best to remain flexible. And they decided to be proactive about family time. There were still consequences when Raye or her sisters rebelled, but every night at bedtime they spent time with each one of their daughters, reviewing highlights of the day and saying a short prayer. These nightly conversations became treasured times, and the girls usually shared rich, lengthy descriptions of their daily lives.

The family established weekly meetings to air "family business." Meetings never went over 45 minutes, and the family always enjoyed a special dessert and game time or movie night afterward. And at least once a month, they had a significant family outing: bowling, pizza, or hiking—nothing too expensive, just time and activities that promoted togetherness.

Of course, each of their daughters could push their "hot buttons" in different ways from time to time, and Raye's parents didn't always respond as well as they would have liked. But prayer, Bible study, strong friendships, and the investment they made in their family—every day—kept them strong. And so far at least, their combined efforts have kept Raye from any serious rebellion.

Care and Counseling Tips

THE BASICS

Beginning with the "terrible twos" common to toddlers, some amount of rebellion is completely normal throughout childhood and adolescence. Like germinating seeds pushing against the soil, children have to push against something in order to grow.

Rebellion says, "I'm in the time of my life when I'm trying to figure out who I am." Although identity crises are often associated with midlife, for most people identity isn't really set until the mid-20s. So as kids grow, they are nearly always dealing with varying degrees of identity crisis, which for some is just that: a crisis, and at times it brings about rebellion.

Rebellion looks different depending on the child's age and temperament. It almost always involves questioning, argumentation, and/or defiance against authority. It may also include changes in a child's appearance, interests, or group of friends. As children and adolescents seek greater autonomy, they want to make their own decisions, and so a rejection of rules—both household and societal—is normal. That could mean staying out after curfew, cutting classes, or engaging in risky behaviors such as experimenting with alcohol or drugs.

By putting rebellion in its place as a part of normal development, you'll be better equipped to take steps to limit your child's rebellious behavior.

FIRST STEPS

+ Respond, don't react.

Rebellious behavior tends to elicit strong emotions. Whether your child wrecked your car, failed a class, or yelled in your face, take a deep breath and pray. Take a timeout if you need one, and keep praying. If you react out of shock, frustration, or anger, you risk distancing your child and making the situation worse. Doing whatever it takes to calm yourself down so that you can respond with love and grace will go far toward helping your child and healing your relationship.

+ Determine whether the child is rebelling or acting out.

Once you've calmed yourself, you need to discern whether your child is acting rebellious or acting out. There is a difference. Rebellious behavior may indicate that your child may be transitioning to a new stage and is seeking to understand the accompanying expectations. Acting out says, "We have a problem, and I'm trying to tell you about it."

Acting out tends to entail more severe behavior, often rooted in anger. Has there been a big change in your child's life that might lead him or her to act out: a separation or divorce (see Chapter 9, p. 109), a death or other significant loss, a move, a drastic change in friendships? If you can't clearly see the motivation behind your child's rebellious behavior and you suspect that it's more than a search for identity and independence, a therapist might be helpful.

NEXT STEPS

+ Just say no to power struggles.

A rebellious attitude craves a power struggle. It's up to you as the adult to do everything possible to defuse the situation. Try whispering instead of raising your voice. And tell your child what you're willing to do and when—for example, "I'm more than willing to [insert your willingness here] when you stop [insert rebellious behavior here]" or "I'm more than willing to [insert your willingness here] since you [insert appropriate behavior here]."

+ Be clear and consistent, and always follow through.

Stated another way, choose your battles. As much as possible, decide in advance what's negotiable and what's not. For example, you might decide that your child may style his hair any way he wants, but piercings aren't acceptable. As your child grows in age and responsibility, you should have more negotiables than absolutes. Decide with your spouse on these together before you communicate them to your child so you present a unified front; don't leave room for your child to play one parent against the other.

Make punishment a natural and logical consequence of the behavior. For example, if your child neglects his or her homework, he or she won't get time with friends until the next week's homework is done. If your child experiments with alcohol at a party, he or she will stay home next time. Avoid punitive consequences that are unrelated to the behavior and will just drive a larger wedge between you and your child. Whatever the rule and whatever the consequence, always follow through.

+ Make emotions safe.

Rebellious feelings result in rebellious behavior. Some people feel intimidated by strong emotions and try to deny their strength. Instead, during a calm moment, help your child brainstorm positive outlets for negative feelings. For example, when your child feels frustrated, hurt, embarrassed, insecure, or angry, he or she could loudly sing or play an instrument, draw, journal, exercise, play with the family dog, or take a bath. Once your child has calmed down, see if he or she is willing to talk about the negative feelings or experiences.

+ Create support networks.

The struggles of adolescent rebellion often transport parents back to their own adolescence, with all its struggles and insecurities. If you sense this happening, try to let it pass. Remember, you're the adult, and this situation is not about you.

One way to empower yourself as a parent is to develop a support network. Join or start a Bible study with other parents. The Bible is full of stories in which our gracious God disciplines and forgives his rebellious people. Ask trusted friends to pray for or with you for your child and for wisdom. Connect with other parents who share your values, with whom you can be honest and who will encourage you.

Similarly, surround your child with others who will say the things you would say. Your child may not be willing to listen to you, but he or she might take in a similar message offered by youth group leaders, friends' parents, neighbors, or relatives. Your child needs safe people outside the home with whom to process strong feelings.

Home Life

+ Find your sense of humor.

Being an adult can be serious business—tight schedules, looming deadlines, restricted budgets, and stressful situations. Kids want to grow up, but when they see a humorless adult world that intimidates them, it's almost no wonder they rebel. So find your sense of humor (or develop one!), and play with your kids. Wear a funky wig to dinner. Have a water fight or a pillow fight. Get a joke book, and take turns reading your favorites. Play games after homework. Be silly together. Laughter is the best medicine, after all!

+ Spend time together.

You can choose your friends, but God chooses your family. As much as you love your child, sometimes it will feel like a chore to work on getting along. Still, it's necessary, and at first you'll probably need to be more available to your child than he or she is to you. Here are a few tips to get you started:

• Have at least one meal together each day. Make your home a comfortable place your child (and his or her friends) wants to be.

• Arrange for family meetings, and set an agenda with equal time to talk about fun things—such as future family outings—and issues that need airing.

• Declare your home a "safe zone," and tell everyone to hang their bad days at the back door.

• You can even build relational time into consequences for rebellious behavior; if your child needs a physical outlet to work out his or her emotions, go for a bike ride together.

+ Help your child identify and explore interests.

While our identity should truly rest in who God says we are, we often understand ourselves through things we're interested in or good at. A child who feels he or she has no special interests or talents is likelier to engage in rebellious behavior as a means of establishing an identity. With your child, seek out opportunities to try different sports, musical activities, the arts, or sciences. Spend time together exploring topics or activities that intrigue your child. Everyone will benefit!

+ Be your child's biggest fan.

Kids are looking for acceptance and will find it wherever they can. Instead of zeroing in on bad behavior, celebrate the good you see in your child. Remind yourself of all the things you really like about your child. Communicate to your child that you are on his or her team and, in fact, want to be the team's biggest cheerleader! Go out for milkshakes after a big game, bake brownies to mark the end of a project your child has completed, or leave an affirming message on your child's bathroom mirror.

WHEN TO SEEK HELP

The following signs and symptoms may indicate that a child could benefit from further evaluation:

+ You and your child together can't determine the motivation for rebellious behavior.

+ Your child's behavior interferes with everyday activities, such as school.

+ Your child's behavior negatively affects your child and/or others.

+ Your child's behavior has turned destructive.

What Not to Say

✛ "What were you thinking?"

This question, often shouted in anger bordering on disbelief, puts your child on the defensive. The truth is, your child may not have been thinking at all! Fluctuating hormones can cause rapid mood shifts and, in essence, flip a switch that shuts off rational thinking. You do need to get at the motivation for your child's rebellious behavior, but this isn't the way to go about it.

✛ "I can't believe you [fill in the blank]."

Don't be shocked. By anything. Part of the "fun" of rebellious behavior is the reaction it elicits. Believe your child is capable of anything—he or she is, after all, as imperfect and sinful as anyone else. Instead, forgive and love your child through this rough patch in life.

✛ "You're driving me crazy!"

Your response is your responsibility. Don't let your child's behavior get under your skin. If you feel yourself reacting, think, "breathe, pray, breathe, pray." Consciously or subconsciously, your child probably wants to drive you just a little nuts. That's what rebellion is all about. Consider whether finding yourself a little off kilter may even help you think differently about how you parent. Use feelings of craziness to get creative.

What to Say

✛ "How's that working for you?"

Whether your child is spinning a whirlwind tantrum or has come home with a tattoo, this quiet question asks him or her to reflect on the impact of the rebellious behavior. Allow your child to calm down, think through the behavior and the rationale for it, and take responsibility for his or her actions.

+ "I like you."

You don't have to like your child's behavior to love your child. Your child is seeking independence, identity, and acceptance. Make sure your child knows you'll accept him or her even when you don't accept the behavior. And while you're at it, if you haven't told your child you love him or her in the last five minutes, say it again.

+ "I forgive you."

The Lord disciplines those he loves, and he always forgives those who repent. When your child eventually apologizes for a rebellious behavior, don't hold the behavior or your feelings about it against him or her. Model grace.

SCRIPTURE HELP

+ **Psalm 25:6-7**
+ **Psalm 32**
+ **Proverbs 1:8-10**
+ **Isaiah 54:13**
+ **Ephesians 6:1-4**

+ **Philippians 2:12-16**
+ **James 1:19-25**
+ **1 Peter 1:13-16**
+ **1 John 3:24**
+ **1 John 5:2-5**

ADDITIONAL RESOURCES

+ Books

Peacemaking for Families: A Biblical Guide to Managing Conflict in Your Home. Ken Sande with Tom Raabe. Carol Stream, IL: Tyndale House Publishers, Inc., 2002.

I'm Not Mad, I Just Hate You!: A New Understanding of Mother-Daughter Conflict. Roni Cohen-Sandler and Michelle Silver. New York: Viking, 1999.

How to Talk So Kids Will Listen and Listen So Kids Will Talk. Adele Faber and Elaine Mazlish. New York: Avon Books, Inc., 1980.

ON-THE-SPOT TIPS

Rebellious behavior looks different for different kids and at different ages. Although not every child will rebel in the following situations, you may find yourself facing one or more of these during your journey as a parent.

+ Skipping school

Even very young children will occasionally skip school, especially if something is out of the ordinary (a friend is sick and missing from the class or a substitute will be teaching). If your child skips school, remain calm. Ask your child to explain why he or she skipped school and whether this has happened before.

If you can get to the root of the situation, help your child own the problem by asking what he or she plans to do about it. Offer suggestions, but don't rush to the rescue. Depending on the severity of the problem and on your child's personality, you may go together to talk with a school authority such as a guidance counselor or teacher. Even then, let your child do most of the talking.

+ Your child doesn't want to go to church.

Of course you want to pass on your values to your child, and you know the God who loves your child most will help him or her deal with all of life's curveballs. If you find yourself in this situation, try to determine why your child has lost interest in church. Maybe social issues have developed among peers at church or your child has been subject to verbal attacks at school for being the "lone ranger" Christian. Maybe your child really has heard every Bible story possible, and it's time to start teaching him or her in a new way (using devotional or practical life application rather than stories, for example).

Ultimately, your child's relationship with God is about more than church attendance. Do what you can to uplift the value of church attendance by communicating how much you enjoy church, meeting your friends there, receiving and giving encouragement, and so on, but don't make church attendance the hill you choose to die on. If you've raised your child in church, continue to model church attendance, and pray continuously for God's work in your child's life, he or she will likely come back to it.

+ Personal choices

Rebellion often manifests itself in personal choices such as music or appearance. As much as it might go against the very fiber of your being, remember that your child has the right to make personal choices. You can limit those choices (certain artists may be off-limits, but not entire genres of music, for example), but it's very unlikely you'll be able to completely change your child's mind about choices that are important to him or her.

If you don't like your child's choices, you can ask him or her to lower the volume so you don't have to experience those choices (music), or you can listen in, ask questions, and possibly learn something new about your child. For example, you might accompany your daughter to the mall for a piercing and ask why she chose to pierce her ear three times, or teasingly ask your son if there's any significance to his shaggy hairstyle. Maintain your cool in this area, and you'll likely maintain your relationship.

+ Temper tantrums

We all have crabby moments, but part of growing up is learning to handle strong feelings so they don't cause serious problems for ourselves or others. If you can't change your child's behavior (and really, you can't; your child's behavior is his or her responsibility), change your child's location. Remove your young child to his or her bedroom (or other location) until he or she regains control. Ask older children to remove themselves from the company of others until they can behave more respectfully. Make sure your child knows that by behaving poorly, he or she is making a choice, albeit a poor one. When your child is calm enough to return to polite company, lavish him or her with loving acceptance.

CHAPTER FIVE

Addictions
Offering Love and Support to
Those Who Are Trying to Quit

Marian hated her dad. Why did her parents have to split up anyway? And why did her dad have to get married again to such a goody-goody? At first, it seemed like Joanne was going to be cool. At the wedding, she made a bunch of promises to Marian and her sister, Cori—stuff about being there for them and accepting them. Lies. All lies. If Joanne really accepted them, she would understand that they needed to go out and see their friends, not stay home and watch stupid PG movies with their parents.

Marian wished she could just go live with her mom, Lori. She was much cooler. Lori lived with her boyfriend, and she knew how to have fun. She wasn't home much, but Marian and Cori didn't mind. Lori's absence gave them all the privacy they wanted to hang out with friends. After all, they were teenagers now, not the little girls Joanne remembered from her wedding day.

Joanne looked at the wedding photo on her dresser wistfully. Life was so much easier then. *Being a stepparent to two teenage girls is no picnic,* she thought. She prayed every night that God would give her the wisdom to make wise parenting decisions, and that, although Robert didn't share her faith, they would speak with one voice in setting healthy boundaries for their growing daughters.

Things were going along OK until Marian got her driver's license. Joanne and Robert had placed reasonable restrictions on her car use as she earned her trust as a new driver: No driving at night, only one friend in the car, no driving to parties where alcohol might be served.

Marian laughed when she heard the new "rules." *As if*, she thought. *If they think restricting my driving is going to stop me from partying, they have another think coming.* In her first month of driving, Marian violated Joanne and Robert's "car rules" as often as possible without getting caught. Then one night, after Joanne and Robert were in bed, they heard loud voices outside. Through the open window, they could smell the unmistakable odor of marijuana smoke. The concerned parents rushed downstairs, broke up their daughter's party, and sent her to her room.

Of course, this just made Marian more determined to rebel, and the next time she invited her younger sister to join her. All that summer they drank and partied every chance they got. Of course, there were more chances at their mom's. Sometimes Lori even shared drinks with her daughters, reasoning that if she didn't make a big deal out of drinking, Marian and Cori wouldn't either. Lori was wrong.

Soon Marian and Cori were missing days of work at their summer jobs. They would come home late, wake up hung over, and decide not to go anywhere. When school started, they cut classes almost daily. Their grades dropped from above average to flunking most subjects. Daily screaming matches ensued between Robert and his daughters. Eventually the girls refused to live there and insisted on staying only at their mom's. Joanne worried for them, but as the stepparent, she felt helpless to intervene except through continued prayer.

Because she was older, Marian was better able to manage, or at least hide, her behavior. Before long, Cori's drinking had gotten so out of hand that all three parents agreed to send her to an out-of-state boarding school for troubled teens. Cori hated the idea and rebelled even more. But eventually, she had no choice but to go. She tried to seem unaffected by it all, complaining that life at home with Joanne and Robert would have been no fun anyway.

After Cori left, Marian continued to drink. She partied her way through her last year of high school, somehow managing to attain barely passing grades. And then one night, coming home from a party, she heard sirens wailing behind her. Light flooded her car. She felt her heart leap into her throat as she pulled to a stop.

That night, Marian was arrested for driving under the influence of alcohol. Fortunately, she was alone. Even more fortunately, she hadn't had an accident. But her life changed forever. Her parents were forced to pay huge sums of money to the lawyer who defended her in court, money she would one day have to repay. As part of her sentence, she wasn't allowed to leave the state for more than two days. She did get to attend her sister's graduation several months later, but she missed the family's boating vacation that year.

Joanne continues to love and pray for both girls, asking God to use the consequences of boarding school and DUI tickets to keep their attention and prepare them for a fresh start. So far, Marian and Cori are starting to come around more, and Joanne and Robert like it that way.

Care and Counseling Tips

THE BASICS

Unfortunately, teenage drug and alcohol use is far from uncommon. According to the Substance Abuse and Mental Health Services Administration, in 2006 one-third of American teenagers drank alcohol, one-fifth used an illegal drug, and one-sixth smoked cigarettes. On any given day, nearly 8,000 teenagers drank alcohol for the first time, with the peak years for alcohol initiation being 7th or 8th grade. These teens who begin drinking before age 15 are five times more likely to develop an alcohol addiction than those who wait until they are 21. And among teens 15 and older, alcohol is a major factor in auto accidents, murders, and suicides—three leading causes of death for this age group. The statistics are sobering.

Even if your child doesn't use alcohol or illegal drugs, he or she probably knows kids who do. The most commonly used illegal drugs are marijuana (pot), stimulants (cocaine, crack, and speed), LSD, PCP, opiates, heroin, and designer drugs (Ecstasy). But abuse isn't limited to substances that are illegal. Legally available drugs your child may have access to include prescription medications; inhalants (fumes from glues, aerosols, and solvents); and over-the-counter cough, cold, sleep, and diet medications. Many of these are easily found in your home.

As a parent, you may remember your own youthful experimentation with drugs or alcohol. In your mind then, it seemed harmless, but was it? Perhaps you were one of the lucky teens who experimented and then stopped without experiencing significant problems. More often, so-called "innocent" experimentation leads to dependency and moving on to more dangerous drugs that may lead your child to inflict significant harm on himself or herself. Your child may be at greater risk for developing serious alcohol and drug problems if…

- you have a family history of substance abuse.
- your child has experienced depression (past or present).
- your child has low self-esteem or feels as if he or she doesn't fit in.

The information in this chapter will help you assess your child's drug and alcohol habits and support you as you walk with your child out of addiction toward recovery.

FIRST STEPS

If you are concerned that alcohol or drugs are or will be a problem for your child, begin with the following steps. If you know for certain that your child is already using, you may want to skim this section and focus on "Next Steps," which will support you as you help your child quit.

+ Educate yourself.

It's a good idea to know which drugs or behaviors are popular in your area. They can change from time to time, based on the availability of particular substances or the introduction of new activities to the area. You should stay on top of what young people are exposed to. Not sure where to start? Try meeting regularly with people who work with teenagers, such as youth pastors or school staff in your area.

+ Share your views about alcohol early and often.

It's OK to express rules such as "We don't allow illegal drug use, and children in this family are not allowed to drink alcohol." Explain that you have rules about controlled substances because you love your child and want to protect him or her. If you or your church believes that all alcohol use is wrong, say so. If you do choose to drink, do so in moderation. Remember that your actions also carry messages about alcohol use to your child. Don't reach for alcohol anytime you want to unwind. And if you're entertaining, be sure to offer nonalcoholic drinks to children and adults.

+ Know your child's views about alcohol.

Ask your child what he or she knows about alcohol and why he or she thinks people drink. Hear your child out, without interrupting. Then be prepared to answer his or her questions.

+ Talk about media's portrayal of alcohol.

The media often portray alcohol as glamorous and the people who consume it as happy and popular. Make a point of discussing—and dispelling—this

SUBSTANCE ABUSE & YOUNG CHILDREN

Even if your child is under 12, it's not too soon to start educating him or her about the pitfalls of substance abuse. National studies show that the average age when a child first tries alcohol may be as young as 11 years. If your younger child has ever had medication for strep throat or an ear infection, he or she already knows something about drugs. This is a good place to start a positive dialogue about controlled substances.

The next time a conversation about medication comes up, try saying to your young child, "The doctor wants you to take this medicine to help your body feel better. We only take medicine that the doctor tells us to take. Taking medicines the doctor didn't give us or taking medicine when we're not sick can hurt our bodies. God made our bodies, and he wants us to keep them safe and healthy." You may also want to highlight other things your child can do to keep his or her body healthy, such as brushing teeth, exercising, eating nutritious foods, and getting enough sleep.

incorrect view as you watch TV or movies with your child. Point out that, counter to what the media portray, alcohol is a depressant, and it can make people feel sad or angry. When drunk in excess, alcohol can have serious or even fatal consequences such as auto accidents or date rape.

+ Focus on friendships.

Help your child understand that good friends respect each other's values and choices. Healthy activities such as sports, clubs, performing arts, and youth group also provide kids with the opportunity to meet peers who share positive interests. Affirm your child's healthy friendships, and remind him or her that "friends" who pressure your child to drink or do drugs aren't really friends at all.

+ Build up your child.

Try spending 15 minutes a day of uninterrupted time with your son or daughter, or, better yet, set aside one day a week to focus extra attention on meeting your child's needs. This can be any day of the week, but it works best if you're consistent. On this day, pick up your child's favorite snacks from the store, run errands for him or her, or do his or her laundry (or another chore). Start and end the day by telling your child, "I love you."

NEXT STEPS

If your child has experimented with alcohol and expressed a desire to quit, start with the following suggestions:

+ Help your child practice saying "no."

Role-play ways your child can stand up to negative peer pressure in this area. Talk about what your child can say or do if a friend offers alcohol to him or her. If your child has trouble thinking of responses, offer a few suggestions. For example, he or she might say, "No, thanks. Let's go skateboard instead" or "I don't drink. I need to keep in shape for gymnastics."

+ Talk straight with your teen about the real effects of alcohol use and abuse:

- **Weight gain.** Alcohol is pure sugar. It slows down the metabolism. Plus, it's frequently consumed at parties where there is also an equally plentiful flow of non-nutritious snack foods.
- **Dehydration.** Most people don't realize that alcohol actually pulls the water right out of you. In fact, this is what causes most hangovers.
- **Impaired judgment.** If your child drinks, he or she will not be able to think as quickly in questionable situations. This is why alcohol is implicated in so many car crashes and date rapes. As inhibitions decrease, your child is also much more likely to make poor decisions.

While these side effects can happen to anyone who drinks, extreme or binge drinking can lead to coma or death. The body can only take so much, and when it passes its threshold, major organ systems can start shutting down. Long-term alcohol use can also have serious effects such as memory loss, heart problems, obesity, premature dementia, and loss of bladder control.

If your child is truly addicted to alcohol or drugs, you and your child have a difficult journey ahead. Recovery from any kind of addiction can be a long road, but these steps can help you support him or her on the way:

+ Understand denial.

If you recognize a potential addiction, but your child doesn't, confront gently and respectfully. Point out inconsistencies or realities that your child would rather not face. Don't argue; the best approach is persistence rather than power.

+ Gather information.

Examine your child's life for problems that may drive a need to flee from reality. Assess the level of substance use. Determine which behaviors came first and under what circumstances. The more information you gather, the better you can appreciate your child's situation and help him or her feel understood.

+ Make a relapse-prevention plan.

After identifying situations that might put your child at risk, help him or her come up with a written plan to avoid them. For example, if your child is abusing alcohol, you may need to lock away or remove any alcohol in your home. A drug addict may need to avoid situations where he or she can easily obtain a large amount of cash so the drug will not be easily accessible. The more built-in accountability, the better.

+ Surround with support.

Help your child form relationships with other kids of similar age who are in recovery. Finding 12-step programs in your area is easy; see the "Additional Resources" section in this chapter for websites. You can also contact local churches; many meetings take place in churches. Also promote healthy relationships with other friends at church or school who don't share the addiction. These connections can help your child spend his or her time on more productive activities.

+ Understand relapse.

Many addiction-treatment professionals agree that relapse is an expected part of recovery. The temptation to relapse doesn't represent failure. Help your child deal with the painful realization that the temptation will always be present. Offer ongoing accountability as a symbol of your long-term dedication to his or her recovery.

SCRIPTURE HELP

+ **Psalm 26:2-3**
+ **Psalm 37:5**
+ **Psalm 139:23-24**
+ **Proverbs 16:3**
+ **Proverbs 20:1**

+ **Ephesians 5:15-18**
+ **Philippians 4:13**
+ **Colossians 3:1-2**
+ **Titus 2:6-7**
+ **1 Peter 4:1-4**

WHEN TO SEEK HELP

Seek help immediately if...

+ Your child's addiction has become physically dangerous.

+ Your child's addiction significantly impairs relationships.

+ You observe withdrawal symptoms, or your child acknowledges them.

+ Your child begins to experience depression or anxiety after stopping the drug or alcohol use.

Home Life

+ Reach out.

Witnessing the damaging effects of addiction can leave any parent feeling helpless and alone. But God does not leave us comfortless. As a group, God has blessed Christians with the unifying power of faith and hope that comes only through his love. As you reach out to your struggling child, remember to lean on other Christian friends and family members for support.

+ Stand guard.

Your child will have a long road to recovery once he or she sees the light. Be prepared to make yourself available to your child at all hours. With your spouse (and other family members, if appropriate) sign up for different "posts" that include both night and day. Though the experience will be harrowing, God will bless your commitment.

+ Pray. Pray. Pray.

If you've heard it once, you've heard it a hundred times: Christians are called upon to pray in times of trial! Make use of this unique power by establishing a prayer chain for your child. Ask everyone who cares for your child to join you. Remember: Pray without ceasing!

+ Welcome your child back to the world.

If your child has spent a long time struggling with his or her addiction, he or she will have a difficult time adjusting to a life that doesn't include alcohol or drugs. Encouraging a healthy lifestyle during the transition will go a long way toward promoting a long-term change. Within your family, commit to spending active time with your child, enjoying fun activities such as going to the movies, cooking dinner, exercising, or volunteering. Invite your child's friends to join you!

What Not to Say

+ "Addiction is a spiritual disease; you must not be right with God."

Although many people who recover from addiction do find that spiritual growth is a key part of the process, it's not fair to tell your child that addiction is *only* a spiritual disease. Your hurting child may be working hard on his or her spiritual life, but other biological and emotional factors may be interfering.

+ "Just stop."

Saying this shows a misunderstanding of the nature of addiction. Alcohol and drugs are powerful substances, and beating an addiction is no small feat.

+ "You really shouldn't be doing drugs."

Most likely, if you've raised your child in a Christian home, he or she will recognize that using drugs or alcohol is wrong. Statements like this will alienate your child and will ultimately defeat your purpose of helping him or her overcome the addiction.

What to Say

+ "I care about you."

Use language that is direct and personal. Your child will remember your compassion, even if he or she refuses to acknowledge it.

+ "We are praying for you."

Say this and mean it. Making use of the power of prayer over addiction is the smartest move you can make. Letting your child know you're praying will open his or her eyes to how valuable he or she is—to you and to God.

✚ "This situation is not too big for God."

Addiction can feel overwhelming and suffocating. Those who struggle with it will certainly doubt that God's power is strong enough. Reassure your child with compassion, not with judgment.

FINDING A 12-STEP GROUP

To find a local 12-step group, check with local churches (many meetings take place in churches), log on to www.alcoholics-anonymous .org, or write General Service Office, Box 459, Grand Central Station, New York, NY, 10163, for a list of AA-approved groups.

ADDITIONAL RESOURCES

✚ Books

Alcoholics Anonymous Big Book, Fourth Edition. Alcoholics Anonymous World Services, Inc., 2001. (You can also find the big book online at the AA website listed below.)

Drugs, Society, and Human Behavior, Twelfth Edition. Oakley Ray and Charles Ksir. Boston: McGraw-Hill, 2008.

✚ Online Resources

www.alcoholics-anonymous.org (Alcoholics Anonymous)

www.na.org (Narcotics Anonymous)

www.focusas.com/alcohol.html (Focus Adolescent Services)

www.oas.samhsa.gov (U.S. Department of Health and Human Services)

www.surgeongeneral.gov/topics/underagedrinking/calltoaction.pdf (The Surgeon General's Call to Action to Prevent and Reduce Underage Drinking)

CHAPTER SIX

Unmotivated Child
Helping to Motivate Your Child

By the time Shana got to high school, her parents had been divorced for six years. She said she was used to it, that it was better than the fighting she remembered from early childhood. Except that when her parents were still living under one roof, at least her dad was around sometimes. Now he wasn't around at all, ever.

Shana's older sister had some issues, too. Shana always did what others expected, but Stacey did what she wanted, when she wanted, however she wanted. Shana loved Stacey and thought maybe Stacey's bad behavior made Shana look better than she felt.

Shana's mom, Donna, did her best to hold things together, but she had to work as much overtime as she could to make ends meet. She wished the girls' father would do more, but, well, what could she do about it? Stacey was a handful, but she hadn't gotten into any serious trouble, at least not yet. No car wrecks, no drugs (that her mom knew of), no "bad boy" boyfriends. Stacey didn't even break curfew regularly. No, Donna's newest concern was Shana.

Pete, the high school director at the church Shana attended, had called recently. Shana's small group leader had some concerns. Shana had stopped smiling. On the infrequent occasions when she asked for prayer, her prayer requests centered on her falling grades. She said she really didn't even care anymore. She didn't interact with the other girls like they interacted with each other. Even in the wide range of "normal" adolescent behavior, Shana just seemed a little off, maybe depressed. Had Donna noticed something different about Shana lately?

As Donna thought about her youngest daughter, she realized that Shana had been sleeping more and eating less. Had she lost weight? She was slender, but come to think of it, she didn't normally wear a belt with the pants she had worn to school that day. She had kept up her participation on the swim team, an activity she'd enjoyed for years, but not much else. Donna had assumed Shana was still getting her school assignments done and turned in; she had always been such a good student. Busy with her own responsibilities, Donna hadn't been as diligent about checking in with Shana. She hadn't realized how quickly things could change.

That night while Stacey was at a study group, Donna took advantage of the time to talk with Shana. Shana was resistant at first, but Donna didn't give up. Eventually Shana pulled a progress report from her backpack. Donna felt shocked to see that Shana, formerly a straight-A student, had allowed her grades to slip below C's across the board. Anger and frustration got the best of Donna, and the conversation didn't end as well as she had hoped.

Donna made an appointment with Pete, who explained some of the transitions young adolescents experience socially, emotionally, physically, mentally, and even spiritually. That last one didn't mean too much to Donna, since she didn't attend church. But she appreciated that these people cared enough about her daughter to notice that something was going on, so she kept listening. Pete helped Donna realize that the high school experience can be completely different from that of middle school, and that while Shana might be ready for new responsibilities, she also needed more supervision to manage those responsibilities.

When Donna took Shana out for a snack after school, they had a much better conversation. Together they made a list of assignments Shana needed to work on for each class and divided each assignment into steps. When they got home, they made a wall chart that included the assignments, steps, and Shana's other responsibilities around the house. They made similar charts for Donna and Stacey, too.

But they weren't consistent. They each got busy and forgot to fill in the charts. Then the charts got to be out-of-date, and it seemed like too much work to create new ones. Within weeks the charts were in the trash, and Shana wouldn't get off the couch. She skipped swim practice and rarely went to church. Shana's small group leader took her out for a walk and called Pete as soon as she got home. She now suspected that Shana could be suicidal.

No parent wants that phone call, but Pete called Donna immediately. He and Shana's small group leader came over together. The four of them sat on the living room floor and talked, cried, and prayed together. Shana promised she wouldn't do anything drastic that night; she said she didn't have the energy anyway. And the next day Pete gave Donna the phone number of a family therapist.

With the support of the therapist, her mom, sister, and church, Shana regained her will to live. With her therapist's encouragement, she got more involved in activities, both at school and church. She and Stacey set aside study time each evening; having someone studying nearby, even if it was a different subject, kept her going. They posted new charts, too, and this time they kept them up-to-date, surprised at how helpful it was to have a visual record of their achievements. The family even enjoyed treats together when someone could check off a certain number of boxes: ice cream for Shana, brownies for Stacey, frozen yogurt for Donna.

A church friend heard Shana humming along to the radio and asked why she didn't join the choir. As it turned out, Shana had an extraordinary voice, and she was soon singing solos in worship services. She joined choir at school, too, and the affirmation she received bolstered her self-esteem and brought her a sense of purpose she hadn't known was possible. Donna started attending church, at first to hear her daughter sing, but also because she saw the love people had expressed for Shana.

Now that Shana's in college, Shana and Donna look back at her first year of high school as a very scary memory. They thank God for the church and for others who were looking out for them when they needed it most. And they praise him for the joy they have in Jesus, who walks with them through every day, whether it's a good day or a bad one.

Care and Counseling Tips

THE BASICS

Motivation gets us off the couch to do something. The desire to be strong and healthy motivates us to eat well and exercise. The desire to perform well in school or music motivates us to study or practice. The desire for money motivates us to work. We can be intrinsically motivated, meaning the desires come from within, such as the desire to pursue a hobby just for the fun of it; or we can be extrinsically motivated, meaning we require outside motivation, such as some sort of reward. Someone who is physically, emotionally, and spiritually healthy will be motivated—intrinsically, extrinsically, or both—to achieve something.

Lack of motivation, then, is really a symptom of a deeper problem or problems that you will need to discover with your child. It could be a result of low self-esteem, depression, illness, a learning disorder, a response to a social environment, or a learned behavior.

FIRST STEPS

+ **Do a self-check.**

The first step in helping your child get motivated is to take an honest, humble, and prayerful look at yourself. Try asking these questions:

- What am I/are we modeling in our marriage, relationships, work ethic, stress, and use of technology?
- Do I have appropriate expectations for my child based on his or her age, abilities, and personality type?
- Have I been overly influenced by cultural messages of achievement?
- Do I motivate, reinforce, and affirm?
- Do I understand how my child best receives motivation?

+ **Monitor motivation.**

Help your child identify the areas in which he or she is unmotivated and why. Is your child unmotivated in math but keeping pace in history?

SCRIPTURE HELP

+ **Deuteronomy 6:3-9**
+ **Psalm 26:2-3**
+ **Psalm 55:22**
+ **Proverbs 16:2-3**
+ **Isaiah 40:28-31**
+ **Isaiah 41:10**
+ **Jeremiah 17:10**
+ **Micah 6:8**
+ **John 10:10**
+ **Ephesians 2:9-10**
+ **1 Thessalonians 2:4**
+ **James 4:2-3, 7-10**

Unmotivated in school but never misses a workout? Or does he or she demonstrate a lack of motivation across the board?

Figuring out why your child is unmotivated can be much more complicated. Try these steps to root out the cause.

+ Get a physical evaluation.

Depression may lead to a lack of motivation. Be sure to let your physician know about sleeping and eating patterns, recurrent illnesses, drastic changes in relationships, or markedly decreased interest in activities that your child has previously enjoyed.

+ Get a cognitive evaluation.

Check with your child's teachers first to see if they have noticed anything that might be helpful. Your child's school or physician can refer you to an educational psychologist or other professional who can help determine whether your child has a learning disorder. If you choose to make an appointment with a therapist, visit by yourself before taking your child. The therapist may be able to advise you on some changes to try at home before you bring in your child.

+ Evaluate your child's social environment.

Again, your child's teachers and/or school officials can be helpful. Is your child the target of bullying or intimidation? Boys (especially) who are bullied may find it hard to ask for help because they tend to be embarrassed by the perception that they're incompetent.

+ Get a well-rounded view of your child.

Ask the opinion of teachers, coaches, youth leaders, your child's friends' parents, music or art instructors, child care providers, and anyone else who has access to your child when you're not around. Be willing to hear the truth without feeling defensive. This is about getting help for your child; it's not a reflection of you as a parent or human being.

NEXT STEPS

Demonstrate the following techniques to your unmotivated child:

+ Teach "progressive appreciation."

Today's culture teaches "instant gratification." You'll need to work hard as a family to teach "progressive appreciation" instead.

Have each person in the family set goals and action steps necessary to achieve those goals. Make a chart to keep track of each person's goals that includes a list of both intrinsic and extrinsic motivations. For example, if your child's goal is to pass science class, action steps could include making flash cards, finding a study partner, and studying for a set amount of time each day. Intrinsic motivators could be the desire to pass, the desire to keep up with classmates, or the desire to take an elective course instead of remedial science next year. Extrinsic motivators could include a fun snack during each study session and a new music CD when your child passes the class. Set a time each day or week to review goals, action steps, and motivation together.

+ Help your child explore his or her interests.

Some gifted children lack academic motivation because they're bored. School doesn't provide the stimulation they need to maintain their interest. If you suspect this might be the case, ask your child what you might do together to pique his or her interest. For example, if your child is studying state history, you could visit your local historical society or museums featuring exhibits about your state and research your state's contributions to our country. Check with your child's teachers for other creative ideas. They may not have time or resources to dream up class projects, but chances are they'll be receptive to additional input from you and your child, especially if it motivates your child to keep up with class assignments.

✚ Encourage time with God.

God lovingly and purposefully created your child to be a unique individual who will add his or her own creative contributions to the world. Encourage your child to plug into church activities and to build relationships with others who will help him or her experience the joy of following Christ. Help your child spend time in God's Word and prayer. Consider completing a spiritual gifts inventory with your child. Identification of giftedness (spiritual or otherwise) may help motivate your child to find greater fulfillment in his or her activities.

WHEN TO SEEK HELP

The following signs and symptoms may indicate that a child could benefit from further evaluation:

✚ The child has had a sudden and significant drop in motivation that interferes with school or other major responsibilities.

✚ The child's lack of motivation has continued and/or increased during a six-month period.

✚ The child is self-medicating.

✚ The child has suicidal thoughts.

If your child's motivation problem hasn't reached an urgent stage, then put plans in place to make changes in the home. If you see positive change in your child's motivation within four to six weeks, keep going and re-evaluate the situation in two to three months.

Home Life

✛ Start asking and stop lecturing.

Don't assume you have all the answers. Your child may have a lot to teach you. And even if you do know the answer, your child will learn to problem solve as he or she wrestles with your good questions. If you ask in advance, your child will have time to think situations through and plan ahead.

✛ Recognize the impact of your words.

Which would you rather hear: "You'll never get into college with grades like those!" or "What kind of grades do you think you'll need to get into the college you would like to attend?" The first statement is condemnatory. The second invites a conversation, opening the door for your child to tell you about the college he or she would like to attend, or even if college is on the horizon at all.

✛ Own your own "stuff."

As a parent, it's likely you have played some role in your child's lack of motivation, whether from unrealistic expectations, applying too much pressure, or not listening well enough. If that's the case, humbly asking your child for forgiveness can go a long way toward inspiring your child to take charge of his or her motivation. Try this forgiveness formula: "I'm so sorry I [blank]. I imagine that made you feel [blank]. From now on I will [blank] differently. Will you forgive me?"

✛ Don't rescue.

This can be tough on parents, but you have to let your child experience the full consequences of his or her actions (or lack thereof). If your child forgot to pack a lunch or return library books, don't rush to school with these items. If your child chooses to go to bed late, don't let him or her sleep through first period. You wouldn't do your child's homework for him or her, would you? Let your child occasionally be hungry or tired or get a bad grade. If your child never experiences natural consequences, he or she will quickly learn to let you do all the work.

+ Be responsible together.

Responsibility isn't always easy, but it is necessary. Like exercise, responsibility sometimes gets easier the more we act on it. Make sure your child knows about the authority figures in your life—your employer, your direct supervisor, and ultimately, God—and what you do to show your responsibility to them. Talk about times it's easy and times it's hard. Let your child ask you questions about how you get motivated when you just don't feel like doing something. Invite your child to help hold you accountable to your responsibilities, and watch how it affects his or her sense of responsibility.

ADDITIONAL RESOURCES

+ Books

Parenting with Love and Logic: Teaching Children Responsibility. Foster Cline and Jim Fay. Colorado Springs, CO: NavPress, 1990.

Stressed or Depressed: A Practical and Inspirational Guide for Parents of Hurting Teens. Archibald D. Hart and Catherine Hart Weber. Brentwood, TN: Integrity Publishers, 2005.

The Price of Privilege: How Parental Pressure and Material Advantage Are Creating a Generation of Disconnected and Unhappy Kids. Madeline Levine, Ph.D. New York: HarperCollins Publishers, 2006.

Not Much Just Chillin': The Hidden Lives of Middle Schoolers. Linda Perlstein. New York: Farrar, Straus and Giroux, 2003.

+ Online Resources

www.cpyu.org—The Center for Parent and Youth Understanding

What Not to Say

+ "Don't be so lazy!"

Rarely is laziness a real issue. In fact, our society exerts so much pressure to perform that few of us know how to genuinely unwind and relax. Labeling your child won't help.

+ "What's your problem?"

A child who lacks motivation may have a real problem, but this question sounds accusatory. Even if the problem is rooted in a physical, cognitive, or social issue, your child isn't likely to know precisely why he or she is unmotivated. Instead, affirm that the problem is real, and gently and lovingly seek its source together.

+ "You're not the center of the universe."

Your child's actions (or inaction) may make you feel like you need to cater to his or her every whim. However, if you have been catering to your child's lack of motivation, then you—not your child—have communicated that he or she doesn't need to be self-motivated.

What to Say

+ "I believe you're capable."

Let your child know that you're his or her biggest fan. From the smallest tasks to the biggest, applaud your child's efforts to do his or her best.

+ "I'm sorry you feel [blank], but sometimes we all have to do things we don't feel like doing."

This is a little bit of tough love, but it's a truth your child will need to learn sometime (hopefully younger rather than older!). Point out that facts, not feelings, dictate the way the world turns. Provide your child with specific examples of things you frequently must do (household chores, tasks at work) regardless of your level of motivation at the time.

+ "You do your best, and let God do the rest."

Your child isn't perfect and doesn't need to try to be. If your child genuinely tries his or her best and still doesn't win the race, that's OK. God still loves your child, and so will you. God doesn't always work things out the way we want, but God always accepts our best efforts.

+ "Let's do it together."

Teamwork can be a huge motivation. Have you ever considered hiring a professional organizer to help you reduce the clutter in your home? If you have, chances are it wasn't because you felt you were incapable of organizing. Two heads are better than one, and sometimes another person's perspective can help us see things we might otherwise miss. Working with someone on a task that seems daunting can also provide accountability and an extrinsic source of motivation when our intrinsic motivation may be lacking. The same may be true for your child. Simply sitting together to focus on the task at hand can be valuable relational time and may help your child accomplish his or her goals.

MEDIA DIVERSIONS:

Motivation Stoppers or Conversation Starters?

How often have you walked into a room where a TV was on, only to get sucked in by a story line you really didn't care anything about? Or you get on the Internet to check a quick fact and find yourself still there, minutes or even hours later, surfing useless, albeit highly entertaining, sites?

TV, movies, computer games, the Internet: They're not bad in and of themselves. In many regards, they add to our lives. However, they are an easy distraction from other, potentially less interesting pursuits that nevertheless require our attention. What's a parent to do?

+ Set firm limits.

Set a screen-time limit per day, with shorter times during the school week and longer on the weekends. If your child is frequently distracted by computer or video activities, you might even consider offering no time during the school week. For younger children, try giving a certain number of tickets per week (each ticket represents, say, 30 minutes) to "pay" for screen time. To make tracking easier on everyone, set limits that combine all forms of screen time.

+ Keep track of content.

Know what your child is soaking in. Check ratings. Encourage positive alternatives. Say no as often as you feel necessary.

+ Use screen time as an external motivator.

This one won't work for everyone, but it will work for some. Set tighter screen-time limits than you feel are necessary; then use screen time as a reward for other accomplishments. For example, if your child is expected to read for 15 minutes each day, reward him or her with additional screen time for any extra time spent reading or doing homework. Or offer a movie night as a reward for accomplishing a significant goal.

+ Get involved.

Watch your child's favorite show with him or her; then discuss it. Play video games together. Consider allowing only video games that can be played with multiple players, which may help keep your child from isolating himself or herself in an electronic haze. Find age-appropriate Internet sites that match your child's interests, and surf together. Instead of assuming that your child's screen time won't interest you, look at joint viewing as an opportunity to engage in a subject dear to your heart: your child.

CHAPTER SEVEN

Loneliness
Nurturing Your Child's Social Development

Jared

Although he attended Mountain View Cooperative Preschool, Jared was anything but cooperative. His mother, Lisa, was concerned about his development—so much so that she had recently taken Jared, age 3, for a developmental evaluation.

Jared seemed bright, but something about his behavior was just a little off. Other children in his preschool class were beginning to establish friendships, but Jared didn't seem to know how. When other kids built tall towers, Jared wordlessly crashed them down—no apology, not even a look back to survey the response. On the playground, Jared wandered around in the grass or rode a tandem tricycle—alone, since other kids usually avoided him.

Lisa and Jim had recently moved from another state. Lisa missed her old friends, her previous job, and, most of all, her church. She thought the cooperative preschool would be a place to meet friends—for Jared and for herself. In fact, she had turned down a placement for Jared in a school district preschool program, clinging to the ideal of finding her niche in a happy preschool community.

Other parents were friendly at first. But when Lisa started calling to arrange play dates for Jared, the walls went up. "Erin has gymnastics after school." "I have to pick up my older kids, so the transportation would be too complicated." One parent was honest enough to offer the truth: "Grant doesn't really play with Jared at school much."

Nathan

Nathan sighed. Will was sick again. That meant Nathan would be spending lunch and recess alone. Too bad, because he and Will had nearly conquered Nylandia, the country that was warring against Nation of Light.

Every day at recess, Nathan and Will waged fierce battles in their minds, battles that ranged from the Great Oak to the playground's perimeter. Armed with imaginary swords and staffs, they fought their way through the fourth-grade soccer fields and dodge ball games. Soccer was an evil obsession, they agreed, and shrugged off other kids' complaints and insults as they passed by the games.

With Will gone, Nathan knew he would be in for it today. There was one kid in particular who seemed to have it in for him. Byron was a rough-and-tumble kid who had just started at Eagle Creek Elementary this year. He had moved several times and lived with his grandmother. Byron knew just how to annoy Will and Nathan.

Besides insulting Nation of Light (a very serious offense in Nathan's eyes), Byron had chalked untrue graffiti about Will on the school wall. And once he even called Nathan "devil-worshipper." That had been the last straw, forcing Nathan to physically push Byron away, which of course landed them both in the counselor's office.

Every day when Nathan's mom picked him up from school, she was greeted with a litany of "crimes against Nation of Light." When they got home, Nathan would retreat to his room to read, play video games, or dream of tomorrow's battles.

Hopefully, Will would be back soon.

Mara

Mara had always been a sensitive child. Quiet and compassionate, she weathered her parents' divorce and her mother's remarriage. Because of the divorce, Mara had changed schools several times during her elementary and middle school years. She didn't have a lot of close friends, but she seemed to get along well with most kids.

When Mara reached high school age, she applied and was accepted to a local arts-focus school. Mara hoped she would get to meet some other kids who were into art. Her mom, Julie, hoped that Mara would get to stay at the school long enough to build lasting friendships and that she would connect with kids who lived nearby.

At the art school, each student declared a "major." Mara's major was visual arts, or VA as the cool kids liked to call it. Julie frequently referred to Mara affectionately as her "moody artist." If she thought Mara was moody, she should have seen some of the other kids at school. The VA kids actually had a reputation as being more grounded than most. Theater and production majors were mostly a bunch of potheads, and the performing arts crowd was high-strung, anxious, and fussy. For the first time since the divorce, Mara began to feel like she truly fit in at school.

Then something horrible happened. One of Mara's friends died in an accident. The school insisted that Mara attend weekly meetings with a counselor. Mara didn't need any stupid counselor to tell her she was sad about losing her friend. Duh. Every day after school, Mara headed straight for her room. Her hot, stuffy attic room. She used to hate it. Now it was her haven. She painted her feelings about the accident, school, and even the stupid counselor.

After a few weeks, Mara stopped meeting with the counselor. She also stopped going to school sometimes, although she didn't mention this part to her mom. Anytime Julie asked, Mara just shrugged and answered, "You know, that counselor is really stupid, Mom." Pretty soon, the school called to tell Julie that Mara had been marked absent several times. The absences all coincided with days Mara had counselor meetings.

Julie made an appointment with the school. The counselor believed Mara was depressed, possibly even suicidal, and in denial about her friend's death. Julie was devastated to hear this assessment of her daughter. After dinner that night, she had a long conversation with Mara. They talked about Mara's grief, what she missed most about her friend, and what she was doing to deal with her feelings. Julie was relieved to conclude that while Mara may have been mildly depressed, she was certainly not suicidal.

As it turned out, Mara really did have a problem with the counselor. She did need someone to talk to about her feelings, but not someone who would be alarmed by them. Julie arranged for one of Mara's favorite teachers to meet her once a week after school. They played chess, usually, and talked—sometimes about Mara's feelings, sometimes about other things. Mara still missed her friend, but life was better, for Mara and for Julie.

Care and Counseling Tips

THE BASICS

From time to time, all kids experience feelings of isolation and loneliness, especially if they've recently experienced a stressful event such as moving (like Jared), switching schools, a death or loss (like Mara), or the birth of a sibling. However, children experience isolation differently at different ages. Teenagers are notoriously moody, so sometimes it's difficult to determine whether intervention or just plain patience is required. Teenagers engaged in risky behaviors will isolate themselves from parents or even from friends who might disapprove. (See Chapters 2, 4, 5, and 12.) In elementary school, gifted children who lack "true peers" (other children who are on their intellectual and emotional level) often experience isolation. Around the midpoint of the grade school years, kids may begin to form cliques, and children experience isolation when they are excluded, even for trivial reasons.

Isolation in preschoolers happens less frequently and may be cause for concern. Development in the preschool years lays the foundation for social thinking and interacting with others. Many social concerns confront parents and teachers of preschoolers—sharing, hitting, and biting, just to name a few—but isolation usually isn't one of them. Most preschoolers are moving out of parallel play, where they play in proximity to others, to cooperative play, where they seek out and engage the children who are playing around them. Preschoolers who isolate are moving in the opposite direction of typical development and may warrant further evaluation.

Keeping your child afloat on the stormy sea of friendship can be challenging at any age. You want your child to have friends, but try as you might, you cannot choose your child's friends for him or her. You can't force other children to befriend your child, either. However, with careful observation, you may be able to tease out the reasons for your child's isolation.

Causes and treatments for social isolation are many and varied. On one extreme, children with social disabilities such as autism may be isolated to the point that they aren't even aware of other people around them. At the other end of the spectrum, socially savvy bullies may find themselves isolated from peers as a result of physically or verbally abusive behavior. Most cases of isolation fall somewhere between these two extremes. The suggestions in this chapter will help you understand and support your child as he or she struggles with feelings of isolation.

FIRST STEPS

✛ Listen to your child's concerns.

"I don't have any friends" may sound like whining to you, but it represents a real problem for your child. Between school, church, and other activities, your child probably spends close to 40 hours a week in the company of peers. Imagine how you would feel if you went to work every day knowing that no one liked you or wanted to be with you.

Your child needs friends to learn important life skills such as conflict resolution, problem solving, and empathy. Research shows that children who are frequently rejected by peers are more likely to drop out of school or experience other problems later in life. This isn't just kid stuff; it's life stuff, and it's important that you hear your child out and help him or her find effective solutions.

✛ Know your child's temperament.

Researchers have identified nine different traits that make up a person's temperament. These apply to adults as well as children. Consider where your child fits on the temperament spectrum and whether temperament may be a factor in his or her current situation. For example, if one of your child's temperament traits is a low activity level, he or she may actually *need* more time alone and away from the rowdy kids that roam your neighborhood.

While you're at it, think about your own temperament and your spouse's. Does it match your child's, or is it markedly different? Depending on his or her temperament, your child's need for social interaction may be greater or less than your own. Be careful that you aren't setting expectations for your child that his or her God-given temperament has not prepared your child to meet.

Temperament Traits
- **Activity Level**—Is your child quiet or active?
- **Regularity**—Does your child crave routine or go with the flow?
- **First Reactions**—Does your child tend to approach or withdraw in new situations?
- **Adaptability**—How does your child handle changes and transitions?
- **Sensitivity**—How sensitive is your child to light, sound, temperature, and emotion?
- **Intensity**—Does your child laugh and cry loudly or react in a quieter way?
- **Mood**—Is your child more often content or unhappy?
- **Distractibility**—How much is your child distracted by things going on around him or her?
- **Persistence**—Does your child focus intently on a task or interaction, or is his or her attention more fleeting?

✦ Distinguish between social-skills problems and social disorders.

Social-skills problems may be symptoms of more serious disorders, or they may be part of typical development. Typical social-skills problems include bossy behavior, self-centeredness, shyness, poor manners, and bullying (which can become a more serious problem if not addressed promptly). Children who are gifted may also be perceived as lacking social skills since their intellectual development is usually ahead of their social development. Biologically or neurologically based disorders that impact social skills include autism and other developmental disabilities, ADHD, bipolar disorder, and depression. Any of these conditions should be diagnosed and treated in consultation with a qualified mental health professional.

NEXT STEPS

✦ Help your child be the best friend he or she can be.

Although children's perceptions of friendship change as they grow, most children seek friends who are fun to be with, trustworthy, and similar to themselves. Older children and teens may also consider whether friends

SCRIPTURE HELP

+ **Psalm 23**
+ **Psalm 46:1-3**
+ **Psalm 62:1-2**
+ **Psalm 121**
+ **Jeremiah 29:11**
+ **John 14:27**

+ **Romans 8:37-39**
+ **2 Corinthians 1:3-5**
+ **2 Corinthians 4:8-9, 16-18**
+ **1 Peter 4:12-14**

will be positive or negative influences, or whether potential friends would mesh with their existing crowd.

Talk with your child about what he or she is looking for in a friend; then gently help your child walk through a self-check to see how well he or she currently demonstrates those qualities. Praise and encourage your child for friendship skills he or she already demonstrates consistently. If concerns come up, help your child think of practical ways he or she could be friendlier in those areas.

+ Always be on the lookout for potential friends.

If your child seems to be having trouble making friends, be prepared to help him or her. With your child, list potential places where friends might be found. School may be obvious, but what about other places? Your neighborhood; your child's sports, music, or other social activities; and, of course, your church should be at the top of your list. If your child is interested in making friends with a particular child or group of children, call and arrange an outing. Teenagers may be able to do this on their own, with your encouragement. Younger children will require their parents' involvement to set up and carry out this plan.

+ Actively woo your child.

If your child does become isolated, don't let the door slam on your communication. Walk to your child's room and knock on his or her door. Ask your child what he or she is doing. Show genuine interest; even join in if your child is willing. Spend time talking with your child about his or her feelings of isolation. Let your child know that you care, and ask how you can help.

+ Help your child find perspective.

Isolation has the potential to become a self-fulfilling prophecy. If your child seems stuck in a negative cycle, break through by reminding your child of all the people who like him or her—starting with you!

Encourage your child to turn to God for comfort and strength. In our pluralistic society, sometimes kids may feel isolated because of their faith. Especially if this is your child's experience, share examples from the Bible of people who turned to God when they felt alone. (Examples include David being chased by Saul; Ruth leaving her home and family; and Job losing everything, including the understanding of his friends.)

ADDITIONAL RESOURCES

+ Books

Problem Child or Quirky Kid? A Commonsense Guide for Parents. Rita Sommers-Flanagan and John Sommers-Flanagan. Minneapolis, MN: Free Spirit Publishing, 2002.

Helping the Child Who Doesn't Fit In. Stephen Nowicki, Jr. and Marshall P. Duke. Atlanta, GA: Peachtree Publishers, 1992.

Good Friends Are Hard to Find: Help Your Child Find, Make, and Keep Friends. Fred Frankel. Los Angeles, CA: Perspective Publishing, 1996.

The Challenging Child: Understanding, Raising, and Enjoying the Five "Difficult" Types of Children. Stanley I. Greenspan. New York: Da Capo Press, 1995.

Pathways to Competence: Encouraging Healthy Social and Emotional Development in Young Children. Sarah Landy. Baltimore, MD: Paul H. Brookes, 2002.

Home Life

+ Practice relationship skills within your family.

Getting along and making friends can start right in your home. Model healthy family communication. Let your child see you and your spouse disagree agreeably. Encourage siblings to try to resolve their own conflicts. If they get stuck, offer to mediate but not to solve the problem.

+ Make your home a place in which your child's friends will want to hang out.

Make sure you have a variety of activities that kids can do together. (For younger children, consider stocking duplicates of your child's favorites to encourage easier sharing.) Board games, outdoor games, action figures, or other imaginative play toys work well up through elementary school. Stock your pantry and refrigerator with your child's favorite snacks. When your child's friends come over, encourage your child to share generously. (You may need to buy extra for teenage boys, who are often voracious eaters!)

If your teenager frequently chooses video games, make sure you have at least a couple of games that have a two-player mode. Make sure your teen has enough privacy when friends come over—don't let pestering younger siblings sabotage this quality friendship time. Greet your teenager's friends cordially, and then move on with your usual routine (or, if necessary, to an entertaining activity you've planned for your younger children). Quick questions or comments such as "How's basketball going?" or "Great article in last week's school paper" can help your child and his or her friend feel at ease.

+ Check in with your child daily.

By setting and keeping a regular touch-base time, you communicate to your child that you are always available for him or her. Whether you chat over cookies after school or stop in the doorway at bedtime, your child will appreciate your undivided attention, even if it's only for 10 or 15 minutes.

And by keeping tabs on your child, you'll be able to recognize isolation and offer support right away if it appears.

+ Get to know the families of your child's friends.
It's much easier to arrange spur-of-the-moment outings if you're already comfortable with your child's friends' parents. Grab a cup of coffee after you drop the kids off at school. For younger kids, arrive early at pick-up time and wait where parents frequently gather. Or do something extravagant and invite an entire family to join you for dinner, either in your home or at a casual restaurant. You may even find a new friend in the process.

WHEN TO SEEK HELP

Seek help immediately…
+ If you or your spouse has experienced depression or another significant mental-health concern.
Children don't compartmentalize the way adults do. Even if your depression has passed, your child may have internalized his or her response to it. And if you're still dealing with your own depression, you'll need support to help your child.
+ If you believe your child is using drugs or alcohol.
Feelings of isolation may cause kids to experiment with or abuse drugs. But the reverse can also happen: Even low-level drug use can sometimes create symptoms of depression. A professional can help differentiate between these situations.
+ If your younger child begins to withdraw socially or demonstrates a lack of interest in or curiosity about his or her environment.
+ If your child's normal eating or sleeping patterns are consistently disrupted.
+ If your child talks about suicide or wanting to harm himself or herself.
(See Chapter 1, page 7, for more information about suicide.)

What Not to Say

✦ "You do, too, have friends."
Your lonely child needs your support, not an argument. If your child complains that he or she doesn't have any friends, accept this assessment as valid—at least in your child's mind. Instead of arguing the point, try asking your child to name kids he or she plays or hangs out with during unstructured times such as lunch, recess, or free periods. Some of these kids might be friends, or at least potential friends.

✦ "Snap out of it."
Rarely does a child choose to be miserable. If conquering feelings of isolation were as easy as "snapping out of it," your child would have done it by now. Think before you speak, and offer comfort to your child the way you would like to be comforted in your own times of loneliness.

✦ "Maybe you just need to try harder."
If your child is experiencing isolation, most likely he or she has already tried very hard to make friends. Instead of telling your child to try harder, help your child try approaching friendship in a different way, such as looking for friends in different settings, giving more compliments, or changing the way he or she greets kids in the halls.

What to Say

✦ "How can I help?"
This statement lets your child know you're available but at the same time encourages him or her to take action rather than feeling sorry for himself or herself. Listen to your child's ideas, and agree on one that you'll work on together this week.

+ "We all feel lonely sometimes."

It's hard to keep feeling lonely when you know you're not alone. Share with your child times you've felt lonely and the strategies you used to comfort yourself. Younger children especially like to hear about your experiences when you were their age. If your teenager rolls his or her eyes at this approach, try focusing on more current situations. For example, you might feel lonely when your spouse travels on a business trip or while your teenager is away at summer camp. This will help your teenager see that loneliness isn't something that affects only him or her and that it doesn't have to be all-consuming.

+ "How have you been praying about this?"

Times of loneliness can be times of growth in your child's prayer life. If your child hasn't yet considered praying about the situation, invite him or her to try it. If the situation isn't too severe, encourage your child to consider whether God might be teaching him or her to trust and wait. If your child is willing, commit to pray with him or her about the situation, or find another prayer buddy to come alongside your child during this time.

CHAPTER **EIGHT**

Stress and Anxiety
Helping Your Child Cope With Stress

When Tomas started sixth grade, he was flying high. The new middle school seemed to be perfect for him: small classes; caring, communicative teachers; and a comfortable, homelike atmosphere. Although he missed the friends he had left behind in elementary school, he definitely did *not* miss the fifth-grade teacher who had nearly ruined his self-esteem.

Everything was going relatively well until it happened. One day, while Tomas was innocently eating his lunch, enjoying a warm fall day outside with his developing friends, trouble flew in. As he sipped his pineapple juice, a wasp crawled out and stung him on the lip. He sputtered and coughed, screamed, and then ran inside. Teachers tended to the sting. Tomas rested until his mom came to pick him up. On the way home, he threw up. And that was the beginning.

From that point on, Tomas' worry kicked into high gear. He still worried about all the usual stuff, like getting his homework done and making new friends. But he also worried about going outside. He worried about wearing clothes that might attract insects. And most of all, he worried about throwing up again.

Each time he stepped into the car, Tomas remembered that horrible day. It seemed to be etched into his mind, even down to the clothes he was wearing. No more jeans, because that's what he was wearing the day of the sting. His green tiger shirt, a prized souvenir from the zoo, was now relegated to a dark corner of the closet. No more pineapple juice either.

"Mom, can I ride in the back?" Tomas asked, first occasionally and then frequently. First longer car trips and then even the familiar 10-minute drive to school became almost unbearable. Only by lying down could he fend off the anxiety, and even then it was difficult.

The snacks he had formerly enjoyed as an energy boost en route to his after-school activities were now loathsome to him. Eat in the car? How could he? At mealtimes, Tomas picked at his food, not wanting to eat too much lest his stomach reject and eject the meal.

His parents had, of course, noticed his growing anxiety. Various friends and family members attributed it to adolescence, the new school, and the stepped-up demands of twice-weekly choir rehearsals. Taken separately, none of these seemed overwhelming. Yet, clearly, something was gnawing at Tomas. He began to have all manner of stomach ills, from excess gas (embarrassing for anyone, but especially a young teen) to cramps, indigestion, and constipation.

A trip to the doctor revealed nothing, other than the news that Tomas had lost nearly 10 pounds from his already slender frame. A trip to the urgent care center in the midst of a severe bout of symptoms proved nearly as fruitless. "Could be irritable bowel," the doctor reported, "but it's hard to tell." Puzzled, Tomas' parents looked for ways to reduce his stress. They moved him out of his Spanish class, which had been a source of conflict for him. They quit carpooling so they could offer him support and encouragement prior to his after-school activities. Still, he didn't improve very much.

When Tomas was sent home from a choir concert due to health concerns, his mother broke down. As she drove to pick up Tomas, she cried out to God. She prayed for Tomas' health, body, and spirit and that the source of his anxiety would be identified so family and friends could better support him.

"I'm sorry I couldn't do the concert, Mom," Tomas said sadly, his head bowed.

"It's OK, Tomas. But we need to figure out what's causing these problems," his mother replied gently.

Later that night, Tomas reluctantly confessed to his mother the anxiety that had overtaken his life. Yes, there was some stress at school as he tried to fit in with a new group of kids. Yes, the choir rehearsals were long and sometimes tiring. But more important, the obsessive fear of throwing up reared its ugly head daily, every time he ate anything or went anywhere.

At that point, Tomas' family knew it was time to seek professional help. Though irrational in its intensity, the fear of throwing up was very real to Tomas, and more than they or he could manage alone. They contacted a psychologist they had seen before, who helped Tomas to better understand and manage his anxiety. Little by little, daily life began to improve. Tomas moved to the front seat—of the car, and of his life. The psychologist helped him "talk back" to his fear so it no longer controlled him.

Tomas' parents also reached out to family and friends, who responded with help and encouragement. Tomas' uncle began a daily e-mail correspondence with him. Teachers modified his schoolwork to allow time for Tomas to rest and catch up. His youth group leaders visited and brought his friends.

In spite of all these things, Tomas still worried and felt he was too busy. He never had time to do the things he wanted to do, he thought. He shared this concern with his mother, who brought out a calendar. Together, they wrote in the dates and times of his existing activities. Then he told his mother what else he really wanted to do: write, enjoy time outdoors, read, and relax. Looking at the calendar helped him realize that he still had time for these things. And it helped his mother understand that although Tomas was growing up, he still needed help to prioritize his available free time.

With all these supports in place, Tomas is better able to manage his anxiety. He still has stress in his life—who doesn't?—but most of the time he keeps it in perspective. In his locker is posted a quote, given to him by his mother before a big concert: "Peace. It does not mean to be in a place where there is no noise, trouble, or hard work. It means to be in the midst of those things and still be calm in your heart." In his heart is a favorite Scripture, Philippians 4:13: "I can do everything through Christ, who gives me strength."

Care and Counseling Tips

THE BASICS

Every one of us experiences stress. As parents, we're more than familiar with that hurried, harried feeling of trying to keep one step ahead of family members' busy schedules. Add to that the stress of deadlines at work, stretching the budget to cover rising expenses, and countless other challenges. For most of us, stress is a familiar, though not necessarily welcome, companion in our daily lives. We recognize stress, deal with it as best we can, and look forward to a time when our stress levels will drop, perhaps upon completion of a big project or event. But let's face it, we're adults. What about kids and stress?

Short-term stress can help us prepare to be at our very best. This is also true for kids. Before a musical performance, a test at school, or a sporting event, many kids experience anxiety that helps them get ready for the challenge ahead. They may experience nervous stomachs, sweaty palms, increased heart rates, and increased blood pressure.

However, as Tomas experienced, a constant state of stress can be physically and psychologically damaging. When kids don't recognize stress or handle it poorly, problems such as high blood pressure, ulcers, or other conditions can result. Many teenagers, and even older elementary-aged kids today encounter stress from several sources: Their bodies are changing rapidly, they feel pressured to succeed in school and other activities, they face increasingly complex social demands from their peers, and they're trying to renegotiate family relationships.

You're probably already aware of many of the stressors your child encounters, but you can help your child learn to handle stress in healthy ways.

FIRST STEPS

The first step in helping your child reduce stress is to help him or her identify where the stress is coming from. It may be obvious to you, but it's important that your child be able to recognize the source for himself or herself. This will greatly aid in independent problem solving and dealing with stress in the future. To simplify the process, you might help your child categorize the situation into external and internal stressors:

+ External stressors

Often an external event creates stress in a child's life. Some examples might include a divorce, friendship or boy-girl relationship issues, a family's relocation to a new area, or a school problem. In some cases, external sources of stress can be changed, but other times they can't. If it seems that your child could have a part in changing his or her situation, ask open-ended questions like "It seems that if there were a way to do it differently, that would be nice for you. What do you think?" If not, help your child accept the situation and adapt to it.

+ Internal stressors

Internal stressors relate to how we think and feel about the everyday events in our lives. Beliefs such as "I'm the least valued member of the team," "No one understands me," and "Nothing will help" all create greater stress when dealing with everyday problems. The good news about internal stressors is that we can change them. Try having your child journal every night before bed. Many internal stressors seem less important when seen on paper.

NEXT STEPS

Demonstrate to your anxious child the following techniques.

+ Teach relaxation and calming techniques.

People can use a number of techniques to relax and calm themselves. Teach your child about visualization (imagining a more peaceful place), distraction (engaging in physical activities when stressed), deep breathing, and muscle relaxation (tightening and relaxing muscle groups). Check out the box on page 108 of this chapter for muscle-relaxation ideas.

+ Encourage journaling.

Research has shown that expressing emotions in writing is an effective way to help people psychologically deal with problems.

SCRIPTURE HELP

+ **Deuteronomy 31:8**
+ **Psalm 27:1**
+ **Psalm 94:18-19**
+ **Psalm 139:23-24**
+ **Proverbs 12:25**

+ **Matthew 6:25-34**
+ **John 14:27**
+ **Philippians 3:12-14**
+ **Philippians 4:4-9**
+ **1 Peter 5:6-7**

+ Encourage prayer.

People with stress and anxiety problems need to know that God is listening and is able to deliver them from any problem. Although God doesn't always deliver them in the way they had in mind, the process of prayer can still be very calming.

+ Recognize unrealistic thinking and expectations.

The cause of upsetting emotions is not so much the events in our lives but how we think about those events. For example, one person may accept that a traffic jam, while frustrating, is beyond his control; another person, seeing the same traffic jam, yells, curses, and gets his blood pressure up. Thinking positively about situations can help reduce stress.

Home Life

+ Sprinkle surprises.

Kind words and gestures can sure brighten a day. Invite family members or friends to write notes of encouragement and mail them to your child when you know he or she will face an especially stressful experience. Include uplifting Bible verses and/or short prayers of support. Prepare your child's favorite meal or snack or a special beverage to sip while doing schoolwork. Slip a funny joke or anecdote in with your child's school lunch. Your creativity is the limit!

+ Clear clutter.

Create a stress-free sanctuary for your child. Include cozy pillows, favorite magazines or other light reading, candles or other soft lighting, soothing music (or loud music if it helps your child release stress), and calming images. Set up this special place in your child's room or somewhere in your home where your child can retreat for private moments during stressful times.

+ Make mealtimes talking times.

Take time each day to sit down and enjoy a meal as a family. If the thought of cooking stresses *you* out, pick up a pizza or other takeout meal. The quality of the food is far less important than the effort you make to truly listen to your child. Ask him or her to tell you the best and worst thing that happened at school. Then brainstorm good things that might result from even difficult experiences.

+ Show your child how to live in the moment.

In our planner-addicted culture, it's all too easy to let future events distress and distract us from enjoying what we're currently doing. For many kids (and parents, too!), the anticipation of a stressful event can be worse than the event itself. Make an agreement with your child (and any other family members who want to participate) to hold each other accountable to stop worry in its tracks by focusing fully on the present. Trust God with the future.

+ Breathe.

Learn about and help your child practice relaxation techniques. We live in a way-too-stressed-out world, and everyone feels it. Pray together, if your child is willing. If not, take time out of your own hectic day to pray for him or her. Meditate on God's Word. Practice deep breathing. Take time out to exercise, to play, to eat, to laugh, to regain perspective—God's perspective!—on life.

+ Divide up all that needs doing, and get to it.

Help your child learn time-management techniques, either with a system that you've used successfully or a new one you'll try together. (Many schools encourage children in fourth through twelfth grades to record daily assignments in a planner, so be sure to check with your child's school or teacher(s) to see if a system is already in place.) Teach your child to set aside time each week (and each day, if possible) to write down what needs doing and what steps he or she will take to accomplish those goals. Encourage your child not to worry about what can't change and to work hard on those things he or she can control.

What Not to Say

+ "Everything will work out just fine."

This statement belittles your child's feelings. While it may (hopefully) be true that things will go well in the end, the overwhelming fear your child is experiencing right now is very real and hard for him or her to see past. If your child's anxiety centers on an upcoming test, a class presentation, or a big game or performance, spending time helping your child prepare may help boost his or her confidence. Otherwise, lending a listening ear may be just what your child needs.

+ "You worry too much."

Do you really want your child worrying about how much he or she worries? This statement gives your child one more thing to worry about. Labeling your child as a "worrywart" may also cause your child to question your loyalty and drive a wedge between you.

+ "God will take care of it."

While your child may know this cognitively, he or she may feel very far from God in this stressful time. Statements like this invite angry responses such as "Well, then why doesn't he?" You want to help your child resolve his or her concerns, not stir up more. To focus on the help you find in your faith, let your child unload his or her concerns, and then offer to pray with and for him or her.

What to Say

+ "Is there anything I can do to help you?"

You can't take the exam or play in the game for your child. But maybe you can help him or her study or bring him or her a special pre- or post-game snack. Just knowing you are willing to help might comfort your child.

+ "How can we make this fun?"

At first, your child may deny that fun and choir practice (soccer practice, homework, housework…fill in your stressor!) could go together. Start by offering an idea of your own. Listen to a special audiobook only when you drive to rehearsals. Stop at a favorite smoothie bar after practice. Instead of doing math problems on paper, use a dry-erase marker and do them on the window. Every 15 minutes, take a joke break. Or a YouTube break! Find a favorite stress-buster and stick to it, or mix it up with fun surprises each time.

+ "Might there be another way to look at things?"

Maybe your child tends to be a "glass is half empty" type of thinker and needs a gentle reminder that the glass is also half full. Dwelling on the negative can make the negative seem so large that it's impossible to see anything positive at all. This assignment might be important now, but will it really determine your child's grade? And will it matter 10 years from now? By asking questions, you can help your child discover the positive—and perspective—in each situation.

+ "Your identity is in God, not the things you do."

Remind your child that God's love is unconditional. As much as you can, show God's love by lavishing patience and compassion on your child. Help your child develop an identity as a child of God and not measure his or her worth by extracurricular activities, grades, or peers' opinions.

WHEN TO SEEK HELP

The following signs and symptoms may indicate that a child is experiencing too much stress and could benefit from further evaluation:

Experiencing severe mood swings, withdrawing from peers, weight loss or gain, trouble in school, crying easily and often, or developing compulsive behaviors (such as hair pulling, face picking, nail biting, or excessive hand washing).

An anxiety disorder is distinguished from normal anxiety by the intensity and frequency of the anxiety, the severity of impairment, and how long the anxiety has been a problem. A clinical diagnosis of any mental disorder is based on a number of symptoms, and only a licensed professional should make a diagnosis. The following signs may indicate an anxiety disorder:

✦ The child's anxiety is the result of a trauma (such as a physical or sexual assault or a car accident).

✦ The anxiety has persisted for at least six months.

✦ The anxiety significantly interferes with school or other major responsibilities.

✦ Obsessions, compulsions, or panic attacks are present.

✦ The child has suicidal thoughts.

ADDITIONAL RESOURCES

✦ Books

The Anxiety and Phobia Workbook. Edmund J. Bourne. Oakland, CA: New Harbinger Publications, Inc., 2005.

The Feeling Good Handbook, Revised Edition. David D. Burns. New York: Plume, 1999.

Life Strategies for Teens. Jay McGraw. New York: Fireside, 2000.

MUSCLE RELAXATION TECHNIQUES

Find a quiet place, and sit or lie in a comfortable position. Tense each muscle group listed below. Hold the tension and concentrate on the feeling for about 10 seconds. Then let go of the tension and concentrate on the relaxed feeling for about 10 seconds.

Face: Tighten the muscles of your face, scrunching up your face, and then relax.

Shoulders: Tighten your shoulders by raising them toward your ears, and then relax.

Chest: Take a deep breath and hold it. Notice the tension in your chest, and then let it out slowly.

Arms: Bring your lower arms up toward your shoulders, tightening the biceps, and then let your arms hang loosely.

Hands: Tighten your hands into fists, and then relax.

Stomach: Tighten your stomach muscles, and then relax.

Legs: Tighten the muscles in your upper legs by raising and holding your legs up, and then relax.

Calves: Pivoting at the ankles, pull your toes up toward your shins, and then relax.

Feet: Tighten your feet as if you were trying to make them into fists, and then relax.

CHAPTER NINE

Divorce
Helping Your Child Adjust to Family Changes

Jane and Julie are sisters. Julie was 9 years old when her parents announced their separation. Jane was 19 and a sophomore in college. Julie and her brothers had no idea their parents' marriage was in trouble. Over the years, Jane had overheard phone calls and late-night "discussions." She knew things weren't perfect but never expected the marriage would end. Although she was away from home, Jane found out about the crisis before her siblings. The reflections below are excerpted from journals kept by Julie and Jane through the years.

October 17 (Jane)
I don't even want to write the words for fear that writing them will bring them into being, make them a reality. But there's really no way to say it except to say it. My mom asked my dad for a divorce. She really did ask him, and she really did have the unmitigated gall to turn my life upside down by telling me.

October 28 (Julie)
Today my parents called a family powwow. This usually means something is up, like maybe a new chore chart. I hoped I wouldn't get stuck with

unloading the dishwasher again. For some reason, Mom and Dad seemed quieter than usual. Then Dad hit us with the news. "Your mother and I have decided to separate."

October 17 (Jane)

How can she destroy our perfect family when I'm a thousand miles away? This is going to wreak havoc on all of us. My brothers and sister are going to cry, and I'm not going to be there. I think that's what breaks my heart most of all. Anguish, hurt, loss, confusion, despair, loneliness. How can they just drop a bomb like that on me and then leave me here alone? At least when everyone else finds out, they'll have each other.

October 28 (Julie)

We were all shocked. How can this be true? Our parents don't fight. My brothers started crying, and so did I. I hid my face in the arm of the chair. I couldn't look at Mom or Dad. Maybe this is just a bad, bad dream. Maybe tomorrow things will be back to normal again.

October 18 (Jane)

I get the lovely responsibility of bearing this on my own. I have friends, but they can't empathize. Even if they have been through divorce—and not many of mine have—their parents are not my parents. Only a brother or sister can share that. I just want something I can smash into a million itty-bitty pieces. Then to somehow grind those pieces into a fine powder. Then to light a fire with the powder and throw a big firecracker into it that will explode so loud that either the world will stop and all the illusions will be shattered or God's attention will be captured and he'll act in a miraculous way.

October 29 (Julie)

I can't believe it. Dad. My dad is leaving. I can't stop crying, and I can't stop Dad from leaving. Our family is falling apart.

October 28 (Jane)

What about my school? Can I even afford to stay here? I am pretty much on my own now, and I intend to stay that way if this goes through. I will not take up permanent residence with either parent. This summer—if I live at home—will be the longest time I ever live there again. Dad has moved out of our house and into his office until he can find another place. So all the kids know now. I've heard varying stories, but the little ones cried a lot, I think.

In Retrospect (Julie, now 29)

I don't remember that time very clearly. I only have a vague recollection of a web of damage. I remember becoming friends with a rough crowd of boys. I remember sitting alone at recess, trying not to cry. I remember wondering whom I could talk to about my home life who might possibly understand. I had splitting earaches, which caused me to miss school. Home alone, I wandered around the house with my hands over my ears, crying my eyes out. I cursed and wondered why no one was there to take care of me. I silently railed at my dad for leaving.

After a while, my dad moved into a house next door to my piano teacher. This bothered me because my piano teacher's studio was always the place I went for refuge from my parents. In fact, my piano teacher was a kind of guardian angel, a constant in the midst of a storm of change. He always asked how I was doing and really listened to my answers. If I tried to hide that I was upset, he gently urged me to talk about it, after which we would bag part of the lesson and just play around and sing.

My brothers and I would have weekly dinners at Dad's, usually pizza and ice cream. I remember feeling very alone because my brothers and my dad always watched sports together. I would go upstairs and cry, unbeknownst to them. I never really felt at home there. It was a very confusing time.

About a year and a half after this separation, my parents suddenly—or so it seemed to me—got back together and burned the divorce papers in celebration. I was skeptical, even cynical.

Sometime between the end of middle school and the beginning of high school marked another painful round of my parents trying to work it out. My dad left again and then came back again. My sister got married, but my parents got divorced. When the divorce finally happened, nearly eight long years later, it was almost a relief. I couldn't stand any more periods of wondering what would happen next.

In Retrospect (Jane, now 39)

True to my word, I spent the summer living in the spare bedroom of a stranger from a friend's church, selling cars for a living. It was so stupid, but I had sealed my own fate by my promise not to take sides by moving back home. It was good to get back to school.

In the aftermath of my family's seemingly surreal situation, I managed to survive. One kind professor brought me flowers. Another all but ordered me to skip class and hit the beach on the days I was most depressed. My friends didn't abandon me in horror. My grades didn't tank. After moping over a perpetually unrequited love interest and engaging in one potentially disastrous fling, I met my future husband. He had no idea that my parents were anything but typically happy—until once again, they weren't. Their inevitable divorce didn't happen until after we'd had the incredible good fortune to get married "during the blip," as we referred to the brief time they had reunited. Younger siblings' weddings (and other family affairs) would not go as smoothly.

Today

It's been more than 10 years since the divorce, and our parents still don't talk much. We're all adults now, married, with a few kids of our own. We try our best to honor both our parents, in their own ways. We still struggle to understand how two likable, intelligent, Christian people could inflict so much pain on each other. The most important thing we've learned is to be as honest as we can and to support each other. And that divorce is lousy.

Care and Counseling Tips

THE BASICS

The changes caused by divorce touch every individual in the family. It's helpful not to view divorce as a single problem or event but instead to focus on the changes caused by divorce (such as living in a single-parent home, losing the noncustodial parent, and changes in routines) and how these changes affect family members. Also, divorce is a loss that must be grieved. Because of their inability to fully understand, process, and deal effectively with divorce and its effects, children's reactions to a divorce are highly dependent on their age and stage in life.

+ Preschoolers and Younger Elementary-Aged Children

This age group usually reacts with feelings of sadness, insecurity, and helplessness. Children may have more tantrums or cry more easily, or they may show changes in their normal eating or sleeping habits. Young children may react more fearfully when separate from parents or may revert to talking baby talk, thumb sucking, or bed-wetting. They may also have increased complaints of physical illnesses such as stomachaches.

+ Upper Elementary-Aged Children

Older children are more likely to express feelings of intense anger and rejection. They may have feelings of loneliness, sadness, loss, and fear or might act as if they don't care. Also be aware that children in this age group may become aggressive, or even hostile, to parents and other adults.

+ Adolescents

Teens who experience divorce are better able to understand the loss, sadness, anger, and pain than their younger siblings. They may express emotions through aggressive actions or might act out, engaging in delinquent or sexually promiscuous behavior. Teenagers may also resort to using alcohol and drugs in response to being depressed and withdrawn. This depression may manifest itself in suicidal thoughts. If a child at any age expresses suicidal thoughts or plans, refer him or her to a mental health professional immediately.

FIRST STEPS

During the initial crisis of a divorce or separation, take these steps with your child:

+ Communicate.

Talk to your child about the divorce. Explain in an age-appropriate way why you're divorcing, and, as much as you know it, convey what will happen next. Especially if you have a hard time being civil with your soon-to-be former spouse, you may want to consider inviting a neutral third party to be with your child during these discussions.

+ Provide a "feeling" vocabulary for your child.

Young children haven't learned all the words to describe the intense feelings they'll experience during this time. Take advantage of everyday experiences to label feelings. Or make a feeling chart (happy, sad, and angry faces), and ask your child to point out how he is feeling throughout the day. Be sure to include mixed feelings such as "happy-sad" or "sad-mad." These can be illustrated with a mouth that is half-smiling and half-frowning. As you talk with your child about these mixed feelings, alternately cover one side of the mouth. Start by talking about your own feelings: "Today I was happy when…, but I was sad when…"

+ Reassure your child that he or she did not cause the divorce.

Children are in a developmental stage in which they think everything revolves around them, so many kids worry that their actions or behaviors caused the upheaval in the family. Continually remind your child that the divorce is not his or her fault.

+ As much as possible, keep your separation low-conflict.

Even if you haven't yet divorced, separation marks a disruption in your

SCRIPTURE HELP

+ **Psalm 27:1-6**
+ **Psalm 51:10-12**
+ **Psalm 121**
+ **Ecclesiastes 3:1-11**
+ **Isaiah 43:2-3**

+ **Jeremiah 29:11**
+ **Romans 8:26**
+ **2 Corinthians 1:3-5**
+ **2 Corinthians 4:7-8**
+ **Philippians 2:12-13**

child's normal routines. Try to cooperate with your child's other parent despite your personal differences. For the sake of your child, look for ways to maintain consistency and keep communication lines open. For example, you could pass a notebook back and forth between visits to keep each other informed about your child's medical needs, school assignments, or upcoming events. As much as possible, try to negotiate conflicts without placing your child in the middle.

NEXT STEPS

As your family continues to adjust after a divorce, stay involved with your child by considering these suggestions:

+ Normalize your child's experience.

It's important for your child to know that he or she is not alone in this pain. If you know older kids, college students, young adults, or adults in your church whose parents are divorced, invite one or more of these people to talk with your child. He or she will be glad to hear from someone who can truly say, "I know how you feel." Your child may also find it helpful to read books (including picture books for younger children) about divorce or other family changes. Here are a few suggestions: for younger kids, *Dinosaurs Divorce: A Guide for Changing Families* by Marc Brown and Laurene Krasny Brown; for older elementary and teens, *Now What Do I Do? A Guide to Help Teenagers With Their Parents' Separation or Divorce* by Lynn Cassella-Kapusinski; for older teens or adult children of divorce, *The Way They Were: Dealing With Your Parents' Divorce After a Lifetime of Marriage* by Brooke Lea Foster.

✦ Help your child find a mentor-friend.

Many children have conflicting feelings about the divorce, the idea of parents dating or remarrying, and visitation schedules. Your child may feel caught in the middle of your two homes. Ask a youth leader, extended family member, or someone in your church to serve as a safe sounding board for your child's concerns. This will allow your child to talk about issues as they arise, rather than keeping them bottled up inside in an attempt to avoid putting either parent in an awkward position.

✦ Find model marriages.

Children of divorce experience anxiety and self-doubt about their ability to establish successful love relationships. Help your older child or teenager identify couples with successful marriages in your church or ministry to model relationships after. Remind your child that every couple experiences problems and that no marriage is perfect, but a successful marriage is possible for him or her in the future.

A "HEALTHY" DIVORCE

Although a divorce is rarely a welcome or positive experience in a person's life, a healthy divorce is possible—one that minimizes the damage to all individuals involved. This outcome is most likely when

✦ both parents remain involved with their child in order to provide a continued sense of family,

✦ both parents work to protect their child from the negative aspects of the divorce, and

✦ each parent is able to accept and integrate the divorce into his or her self-image and future in a healthy way.

Home Life

+ Continue your child's usual activities.

You may have to do a bit more carpooling or rearrange your own schedule, but do your best to maintain your child's schedule of activities. This will provide your child with at least some semblance of normalcy in an unfamiliar, possibly scary time. Familiar activities that your child enjoys can also help shift him or her away from negative thoughts and ward off depression, at least temporarily.

+ Set and maintain boundaries.

Often your child will need to take on more responsibilities at home, but this should not interfere with normal developmental needs. Avoid sharing too much personal information with him or her or putting down the other parent. If you find yourself struggling in this area, find a good friend who can help you "dump" your negative talk before it reaches your child. When you meet with this person, ask him or her to hold you accountable by asking, "Are you ready to stop?" before you close your conversation and go back home.

+ Model self-regulation.

If there is a silver lining to the stormy clouds of divorce, it is that kids can learn how to manage their feelings when it seems as if the bottom is falling out of life. How many adults have mastered this skill? You can help your child (and yourself) by acknowledging the times you let your negative reactions get the best of you. If you've blown up at your child (or in his or her presence), admit it. Let your child know that you goofed yesterday but today will be a different day. Remind your child that you are the parent, and you will handle any problems related to the divorce—one day at a time. Give yourself grace. Remember, adjusting to divorce hardly ever goes really smoothly.

+ Crank up the love quotient.

Express your love for your child in brand-new ways. Take your child someplace special, perhaps a place he or she enjoys but you've never visited together. Create a "wall of fame" to display your child's photos and artwork. Brag about your child's character and accomplishments to friends and family, and let your child hear you!

+ Keep God present in your child's life.

If it's too difficult for you to encounter your former spouse, you may need to find a new church. But don't let the divorce rob you or your child of your faith. Pray with your child. Read a psalm each day, and allow your child to express hurt or frustration in prayer just as David did. Use this situation as an opportunity to teach your child to look for ways God is acting in his or her life, even in the midst of hard times. And if you notice evidence that God is at work, point it out to your child.

WHEN TO SEEK HELP

Consult a mental health professional if you experience any of the following:

+ Your child's response to the divorce begins to interfere with school, social relationships, or behavior.

+ You notice significant changes in your child's sleeping, eating, or self-care habits.

+ Ongoing, damaging conflict is occurring between you and your former spouse.

+ Your child begins to self-isolate or talks about self-destructive or suicidal thoughts or feelings.

+ You feel yourself becoming emotionally dependent on your child.

What Not to Say

+ **"You'll still get to see your mom/dad."**

That's not the point. Your child's life will never be as secure and ordinary as it had been up to this point. For younger children, seeing a noncustodial parent every other weekend seems like an eternity between visits. For an older child or teenager, the divorce will mean managing two sets of household rules, atmospheres, and schedules.

+ **"We'll all be better off."**

Again, this is not the issue from your child's point of view. Your child may feel responsible or at the very least that he or she could have affected the outcome in some way. Even if there have been parental disagreements or trouble in your home, it was still the life your child knew. Change will take time, and adapting will be hard. Your child will never see either parent in the same way again.

+ **"Your dad/mom was wrong to..."**

There isn't one single event or person that caused this divorce. As much as possible, help your child understand that the reason for this divorce is very complex (this may be difficult with very young children). It will be very hard, but don't say anything that demeans your child's other parent. Your child will fare better through this process if he or she is encouraged to love and accept both parents. And by treating your former spouse with civility, you might ultimately fare better, too.

What to Say

+ **"What are your thoughts and feelings about this divorce?"**

It's important for your child to talk about his or her feelings. By phrasing the question this way, you open the door for communication while still maintaining that the fact of the divorce is something you, as adults, have final say over. Anger, hurt, and confusion are natural reactions. It's important to let your child express those emotions to you and others who care about him or her.

+ "I care about you, and so does Jesus."

This break in your family feels like a death to your child, and he or she may feel lost, abandoned, and alone. Even when you're too hurt to comfort your child, Jesus will be there. Teachers may expect your child to keep up, friends may urge him or her to "get over it," but Jesus says, "I am with you always." The stability of Jesus is something your child can count on during this changing time in your family—and for the rest of his or her life.

ADDITIONAL RESOURCES

+ Books

The Blended Family: Achieving Peace and Harmony in the Christian Home. Edward Douglas and Sharon Douglas. Franklin, TN: Providence House Publishers, 2000.

Making Divorce Easier on Your Child: 50 Effective Ways to Help Children Adjust. Nicholas Long and Rex Forehand. Chicago: McGraw Hill, 2002.

When the Vow Breaks: A Survival and Recovery Guide for Christians Facing Divorce. Joseph Warren Kniskern. Nashville: B&H Publishing Group, 1993.

+ Online Resources

www.parentswithoutpartners.org (Parents Without Partners is an international, nonprofit, educational organization devoted to the interests of single parents and their children.)

www.stepfamilies.info (National Stepfamily Resource Center)

www.kidsturn.org (Kids' Turn is a nonprofit organization to help families through parental separation.)

CHAPTER TEN

Self-Destructive Behavior
Understanding What's Behind
Your Child's Self-Destructive Behavior

From the outside, Amanda was a normal teenager. She got good grades, hung out with well-adjusted kids, and was involved in numerous drama and dance activities. However, on the inside, she was caught in a web of depression, pain, and shame. She had suicidal thoughts, so much so that she would write poems about killing herself. Most concerning, however, was that she began engaging in self-destructive behavior.

Amanda's home life was not as "normal" as her outward appearance would suggest. Her stepfather had been sexually abusing her since she was 5 years old. Her mother, Jenny, was verbally and emotionally abusive, a workaholic, and so self-focused that she missed some vital cues that her daughter was on the potentially dangerous path of self-destruction. Jenny also missed these cues because the vast majority of Amanda's self-loathing behavior was done in secret.

To gain a sense of control over her life, Amanda began controlling her eating habits to the point that she entered the beginning stages of an eating disorder. She became a strict vegan without any attempt to supplement her diet with healthy protein combinations. She considered herself fat even though she weighed well below 100 pounds. She bought clothes that were several sizes too large because she had deceived herself that she was gaining weight. However, she relished the attention when others told her she wasn't fat but extremely thin. Ultimately, she spent most of her energy focusing on being in control of her body.

During these tumultuous teen years, Amanda also began the destructive spiral of self-neglect. As a result of the sexual abuse, she was so out of touch with her basic needs that she ceased to engage in basic self-care habits. She would literally forget to take a shower for days on end. She wouldn't brush her teeth for weeks simply because she had stopped being aware of her needs.

Amanda's self-talk was primarily focused on how different, dirty, and horrible she was. In addition, anytime painful feelings began to emerge, she repressed them to avoid facing them. Amanda spent so much time trying to please others during this period in her life that she forgot her own desires, needs, and wants. Most important, she forgot how to feel her own pain.

As the teenage years wore on, Amanda's abuse intensified and escalated. At age 17, Amanda seriously contemplated suicide as she sat in a car outside her Christian counselor's office. She had just begun the counseling that would begin to expose the pain she had repressed for so long. After several sessions, Amanda trusted her counselor enough to start bringing the painful, shameful secrets of her home life into the light. The more she exposed the pain, the less she felt the need to harm her own body.

Over time, through counseling, reading God's Word, and embracing the love of Jesus, Amanda finally broke free of her abusive home life and the self-destructive behaviors that accompanied it. The first step toward healing was naming the abuse. Next, Amanda's counselor made sure that Amanda was no longer being abused and provided her with the courage to confront her perpetrator.

Amanda's counselor provided her with the tools she needed to start taking care of herself. Addressing the shame and self-blame aspect of the abuse was the first step. Once Amanda realized that the abuse was not her fault, she began to feel as if she "deserved" to engage in basic self-care tasks, such as showering regularly. As her self-esteem improved, in part because of a deepening realization of God's love for her, she began to establish healthier eating habits. Her suicidal thoughts all but subsided as she dug deep into Scripture. Scriptures such as Psalm 27:14—"Wait patiently for the Lord. Be brave and courageous. Yes, wait patiently for the Lord"—provided her with hope in what seemed like a hopeless situation.

Amanda's healing took a long time and a lot of patience. It was not formulaic, and it progressed sporadically. However, Amanda did eventually break free from the self-destructive behaviors that dominated her teen years.

WHY DO KIDS ENGAGE IN SELF-MUTILATION?

A study conducted by Armando Favazza and Karen Conterio of 240 chronic self-mutilators found that people engage in cutting because it gives them temporary relief from symptoms such as anxiety, emotional numbness, and thoughts they can't control. Of the 240 surveyed:

• 62 percent reported childhood abuse (50 percent reported sexual abuse),

• 33 percent lost a family member to death,

• 33 percent came from divorced parents,

• 71 percent considered their self-mutilation to be an addiction, and

• the majority described their families as "full of anger…in which they were told to always be strong and prevented from expressing their feelings."

People who don't know how to cope with their deep emotional pain may use self-destructive behavior to find relief, to feel something, to gain a sense of control, or to express their need for help. According to Dr. John Townsend, the author of *Boundaries with Teens*, they may also feel they deserve to be punished, be working to connect with their peers, or be struggling with a chemical imbalance that leads to emotional instability.

Care and Counseling Tips

THE BASICS

Few things haunt parents more than threats to their children. But when a parent discovers that a child's abuse has been self-inflicted, the parent can be stunned. According to the Mayo Clinic, approximately 3 to 5 percent of Americans have intentionally harmed themselves at some point in their lives. And research shows that approximately one in every hundred female adolescents struggles with anorexia. When children hurt themselves, parents who work hard to protect them from outside pain or hurt may find themselves struggling with difficult realities and questions:

"What have I done wrong?"

"Where has this pain come from?"

"What is going to happen to my child?"

If you find yourself in this situation, it may be the most agonizing issue you ever face as a parent. But for the sake of your child, you must put your own strong emotional reactions aside and focus on one thing—helping your child through this.

You and your child may need to deal with difficult realities connected with upbringing, poor choices that you or your child made along the way, and the realities of hurt your child experienced. But there is no help or hope found in paralyzing guilt, rejection of your child, or searching for scapegoats. Rather, sticking with and accepting your child, taking the needed steps, and extending forgiveness to yourself and others involved can make this a defining season in your journey as a parent. This can be the time in which your child begins walking down the road to freedom, and you can help set him or her on that course.

Your child may never respond exactly as you want him or her to, but there is always hope. You and your child *can* overcome self-destructive behaviors. While the choice is ultimately up to your child, you can give your child the tools and help he or she needs to thrive.

FIRST STEPS

+ Honestly evaluate the signs and symptoms.

Although a pierced tongue or nose may be shocking to you, it's not necessarily a sign of self-destructive behavior. Rather, it may be an effort to shock you or to fit in with peers (see Chapter 11, page 133).

But if your child has already exhibited signs of troubling behavior and consistently chooses to wear long-sleeved shirts or pants on warm days, consider whether self-mutilation may be involved. Other signs of this self-destructive behavior may include

- scratches, scars, and signs of puncture wounds;
- burn marks;
- bruises or broken bones;
- well-crafted stories about injuries;
- infections from cuts and injuries;
- isolation or withdrawal; or
- abnormal inability to communicate or express emotions.

Other forms of self-destructive behavior can be manifested in drastic weight loss. These symptoms may point to a problem with anorexia or bulimia. Other signs of eating disorders include

- fatigue and fainting;
- tooth decay;
- spending too much time in the bathroom;
- the cessation of a girl's menstrual cycle;
- refusal to eat, strict eating regimens, or a drastic change in eating habits; or
- fixation on personal physical flaws.

+ Gently and persistently bring the problem to light.

Blowing up at your child or overreacting will reinforce his or her tendency to become isolated and bottle up emotions. Conversely, delicately avoiding the problem will also delay the necessity to deal with it.

Instead, calmly state the facts of the situation as you express your genuine concern. Clearly communicate your unconditional acceptance and love for your child. Share with your teen the common causes of self-destructive behavior, such as the need to deal with significant emotional hurts, the need for control, or the need to feel deeply. While your child may likely pass off this behavior as "nothing" or a sort of experiment, encourage your child to take it seriously, as you do. Encourage your child to consider that self-destructive behavior may be a sign of deeper things in your child's heart that he or she may not even fully understand. Help your child understand that you are going to help him or her find other ways to work through tough emotions—even if it means that *you* have to change the way you react to your child.

NEXT STEPS

+ As well as you can, identify the root cause and the sustaining factors.

There may be obvious issues in your child's past or present that are leading to self-destructive behavior. For example, your child's behavior and demeanor may have changed drastically since your divorce or a death in the family. However, don't try to coerce hidden reasons from your child or try to serve as his or her psychotherapist. Your child may not remember or understand past traumas or difficulties. Suggesting that there must be some sort of trauma may cause your child to feel there is something deeply wrong with him or her.

Consider if your current family culture may be exacerbating or even causing the issue. Prayerfully and humbly determine whether you may have created an environment in which it is difficult for your child to express his or emotions.

+ Include your child as much as possible in your plan of action.

Arm your child with the knowledge of his or her healthy body weight. Help your child reduce self-destructive behavior by teaching and modeling techniques for expressing difficult emotions in healthy ways. Ask your child how you can best help him or her deal with this issue. Gently but persistently refuse to accept responses such as "By leaving me alone."

Resist the temptation to initiate a plan that is highly controlled by parents or guardians. Remember that a need for control is probably contributing to your child's emotional response. Attempting to control your child back to health can lead to tragic results.

Despite your child's objections, it's likely that you'll need to require your child to see a physician and a counselor. Work with your child's counselor to empower your child to make decisions in his or her treatment plan as much as you reasonably can. (Most counselors will support this.) For example, while your child may not have a choice about whether he or she sees a counselor, you can allow your child to choose which counselor he or she sees. As a parent, you may need to override some of your child's choices or desires. But allowing your child to have a say in the process will help him or her have greater ownership in it.

WHEN TO SEEK HELP

✛ Anorexia and bulimia are complex problems.
Self-treatment is nearly impossible. But many people have found freedom and health from this self-destructive behavior through support groups, counselors, or other professional help. If you believe your child is suffering from anorexia or bulimia, get help. Your family will be an integral part of the solution, but an outside professional opinion will help you get started and may help sustain the process.

✛ If other forms of self-destructive behavior such as self-mutilation have caused or have potential to cause serious bodily injury, seek help from a physician who may refer you to a counselor.

If the behavior appears to be less serious, seek help if the problem persists, increases in frequency, or becomes more destructive.

If your child has thoughts of suicide or shows signs of the possibility of suicide, seek help as soon as possible. Refer to Chapter 1 (p. 7) for additional information on suicide.

Home Life

+ Dump downers.

It's easy to feel overwhelmed by the seriousness of the issues you and your child face. Declare at least two days a month as "Downer Dump" days when you and your family put aside the things that bring you down and just have fun together. Go to an amusement park or do something else everyone loves to do (get your child's input on the options). On Downer Dump days, discussions about therapy, issues, and treatment plans are not allowed. Laughter, hugs, and fun are mandatory.

+ Remind your child of the truth.

As you and your child work through the thoughts and feelings behind his or her self-destructive behavior, you'll probably uncover messages, beliefs, and self-talk that are simply untrue. As those lies are brought to light, replace them with truth reminders. With your child, post the truth on your refrigerator, bathroom mirror, or wherever your child will see it. For example, if your child is afraid of being abandoned, you might post a truth reminder that says, "You are never alone" or "For God has said, 'I will never fail you. I will never abandon you'" (Hebrews 13:5b).

+ Provide a weekly time for open resolution.

Set up some basic rules for a weekly touch base that empowers your kids to share their feelings openly. Ask each person to share a least one emotion he or she has felt over the last week. Consider including the following guidelines:

• No one can interrupt the person who is sharing.
• Everyone must use "I feel…when…because" statements when sharing frustrations—for example, "*I feel* frustrated *when* you come into my room without knocking, *because* my room is the only place where I have some privacy."

- While your child's interpretation of the facts may not always be correct, his or her feeling is valid and will be treated as such.
- No swearing, yelling, or defensiveness will be allowed.
- As long as the rules for sharing are followed, everyone will have a chance to participate.

✛ Honestly assess your own behavior.

If your behavior or choices have contributed to or caused the difficulty your child is facing, own up to it. Begin by apologizing to your child and admitting your weaknesses. Then walk in repentance by turning away from and refusing to repeat those mistakes. If you are unable to walk away from the behavior on your own, for the sake of your child and your own health, get help.

Prayerfully consider whether you have created an environment in your home that makes it difficult to express emotions or where demands and expectations are too high. If so, apologize and resolve to do better in this area. Admit to your child that you, too, have issues to work on and that you are striving to change.

Avoid the temptation to shrink back in guilt or fear. We are all broken people, and none of us is beyond the redemptive power and love of Jesus.

SCRIPTURE HELP

- ✛ **Psalm 42:5**
- ✛ **Psalm 116:3b-5**
- ✛ **Psalm 139:13-14**
- ✛ **Psalm 145:13b-14**
- ✛ **Romans 8:1**

- ✛ **Romans 8:35-39**
- ✛ **Romans 15:13**
- ✛ **1 Corinthians 6:19-20**
- ✛ **Ephesians 3:16-19**

What Not to Say

✛ "You're scaring me."

A child who engages in self-destructive behavior usually already has a very fragile sense of self. Expressing shock or horror about your child's behavior reinforces the belief that he or she is isolated, different, and even deserving of the pain your child is inflicting on himself or herself.

✛ "If I find you doing this again..."

Discipline is an important tool in shaping a child's character. Self-destructive behavior, however, is not a character issue. It is an emotional issue. Rules and consequences will not likely force your child back into desired emotional responses. However, it may be appropriate to limit influences that reinforce self-destructive behavior, such as interaction with certain peers, websites, and other media. If you choose to do this, make it very clear to your child that such limitations are not consequences of bad behavior. Help your child understand that you want to help him or her understand and embrace the truth. You need to limit any voices and influences in your child's life that cloud the truth that your child is a unique child of God and worthy of love.

✛ "You're too skinny."

Parents often hope this statement will help their anorexic children understand that their weight loss is excessive. However, statements like these usually do one of two things. First, they bring the focus back to body image and remind the child that appearance is of the utmost importance. If your child is truly struggling with anorexia, the positive intent behind this statement is seldom strong enough to break through the overwhelming messages he or she is constantly telling himself or herself. Second, statements like this reinforce anorexic behavior by making the problem of weight loss the center of attention.

What to Say

+ "I know you've been hurting yourself."

It's painful to acknowledge that your child is engaging in self-destructive behavior. While it may seem easier to hint about your child's behavior, the only effective way to deal with this problem is to face it head-on. Accusations and demands are countereffective. But a humble and honest explanation of the truth can be the first step on the journey toward freedom.

+ "Have you noticed any circumstances, events, or patterns that occur before you react this way?"

According to *A Bright Red Scream* by Marilee Strong, people who habitually participate in self-destructive behavior "almost uniformly report (that)…cutting bouts are generally precipitated by an experience—real or perceived—of loss or abandonment."

Upon reflection, your child may realize that he or she feels the strong urge to engage in self-destructive behavior after the two of you fight, after a perceived slight by peers or teachers, or after other isolating events. Talk with your child about why the event was frustrating. Work with your child to find other means of responding to his or her emotional pain. For example, when the two of you fight, agree together that you'll follow up with each other to work through specific issues within a set amount of time.

+ "Let's get help."

More than ever, your child needs to understand that you are standing with him or her. Tell your child often that you love him or her as much as you ever have and that you're going to walk with him or her through whatever it takes to find healing.

ADDITIONAL RESOURCES

+ Books

Anorexia Nervosa: A Guide to Recovery. Lindsey Hall and Monika Ostroff. Carlsbad, CA: Gurze Books, 1999.

A Bright Red Scream: Self-Mutilation and the Language of Pain. Marilee Strong. New York: Penguin Books, 1998.

Boundaries with Teens: When to Say Yes and How to Say No. Dr. John Townsend. Grand Rapids, MI: Zondervan, 2006.

Parenting Teens with Love and Logic. Foster Cline and Jim Fay. Colorado Springs, CO: Pinon Press, 2006.

When Your Child Is Cutting: A Parent's Guide to Helping Children Overcome Self-Injury. Merry E. McVey-Noble, Sony Khemlani-Patel, and Fugen Neziroglu. Oakland, CA: New Harbinger Publications, 2006.

CHAPTER ELEVEN

Negative Peer Influences
Equipping Your Child to Avoid
Negative Peer Influences

Trevor slammed the front door and walked into the kitchen where his mom was cutting up potatoes for dinner.

"Hi, Trev. How was school?"

"Fine," he mumbled as he rummaged through the refrigerator.

"How did the history test go?"

Gulping down lemonade, he shrugged his shoulders.

Trevor's mom, Cindy, stopped slicing for a moment as she watched Trevor turn and leave the room. "What is up with him lately?" she wondered.

Cindy knew 14-year-olds are sometimes moody, but something about Trevor's moods during the past month gnawed at her. His upbeat personality had turned into a black rain cloud that wouldn't lift. Later that night Cindy asked her husband, Sean, if he had noticed the change in Trevor. Sean agreed that Trevor seemed moodier and distant, but he was sure it was just part of being a teenager.

The next afternoon Cindy waited in the school pick-up lane to take Trevor to a 4:00 dentist appointment. She watched as kids poured out of the front doors of the school. After a few minutes, she saw Trevor come outside with two boys she did not recognize. Trevor and the two other boys were dressed the same—dark T-shirts and dark, sagging pants. "I don't like him dressing like that," Cindy thought as she squeezed the steering wheel.

One of the boys had holes up and down his pant leg and had a tattoo on his arm. The other boy was pencil thin, and his hair was dyed black with a purplish hue. The gnawing feeling inside her intensified as Cindy watched her son. "Who are those boys? Why is Trevor hanging out with them?"

When Trevor got in the car, Cindy tried not to react to the emotions ricocheting around in her like a metal ball bouncing around a pinball machine. Forcing a nonchalance she didn't feel, she said, "So who were those two kids you were hanging out with? I don't think I've ever met them."

"Huh?" Trevor grunted.

"Those two kids you walked out of school with. Who are they?"

"Gerhardt and Brad."

"Oh. So do they live around here?"

"No. Gerhardt lives with his grandmother on the other side of town. I'm not sure where Brad lives. But his mom lets him do whatever he wants. He doesn't even have a curfew."

Cindy clenched her teeth. She knew she should take a deep breath and methodically construct her next sentence, but before she could stop herself, she blurted, "Well, that doesn't sound responsible. I don't want you ever going over to that boy's house."

Trevor thumped his fist on the dashboard. "See! That's exactly like you. You always try to control me. You can't tell me who I can hang out with!"

"That's where you're wrong!" Cindy's voice rose with each word. "We will not allow you to be in situations where there is not a responsible parent."

"You don't even know these people. How can you even say whether they're responsible?"

Cindy and Trevor argued all the way to the dentist's office. When they got home, Trevor went straight to his room and slammed the door.

That night Cindy discussed what had happened with Sean. They both agreed they needed to talk to Trevor about his new friends and decided they would find a time that weekend when the three of them could go out for a cup of coffee and talk about it.

Cindy was relieved that Friday night when Trevor asked if he could go over to Tommy's house. Trevor had played with Tommy all the way through elementary and middle school, and Cindy knew Tommy's family well. "Oh good, maybe he's not hanging out with those other boys anymore," she thought.

"Sure. But you have a soccer game in the morning, so I want you to be in no later than 10:30."

"This season is so stupid. I'm not playing next year," Trevor said as he headed for the front door.

Speechless for a moment, Cindy just stared at Trevor. "But you've always loved soccer," she called after him.

Trevor shrugged.

"Still, you need to be home no later than 10:30."

When Trevor wasn't home that evening by his curfew, Sean called Tommy's house. Tommy's mom told Sean that Trevor wasn't there and that she hadn't seen him all night.

Sean and Cindy were standing in the kitchen discussing what they should do next when Trevor walked in the front door.

"Where were you?" Cindy asked. Her voice was shaking.

"Mom, calm down. It's not a big deal. I'm not that late."

"We talked to Tommy's mom," Sean said.

Trevor flinched. "I knew you wouldn't let me go out with Brad, so I had to tell you I was going to Tommy's. We were just down the street at Brad's friend's house hanging out. No big deal."

"You lied to us!" Cindy looked at Sean for backup.

"This is a big deal, Trevor." Sean's voice was calm but firm. "Distrust has been established. We need to find a plan that will both address the consequences for the distrust and help to re-establish trust. But we're going to wait until tomorrow to discuss this."

The next afternoon Cindy, Sean, and Trevor sat in the living room. They listened to Trevor as he talked about his new friends and why he liked them. Trevor explained that these new friends weren't jerks like some of his old friends tended to be; plus he thought it was really cool how much freedom their parents gave them. Cindy and Sean told Trevor they had seen a change in him over the past month. They talked about ways Trevor might be able to socialize with these kids, including inviting them over to their home. They also talked about how it was important that Trevor stay involved in soccer even though this year's coach wasn't the best.

At the end of the talk, they agreed on some specific privileges Trevor had lost due to his deception, and they also agreed on ways he could re-establish himself as trustworthy. Cindy and Sean both hugged Trevor at the end of their talk.

"We love you," Sean told Trevor. "It's only your behavior we are talking about. You know that, right?"

"Right," Trevor nodded.

Care and Counseling Tips

THE BASICS

Negative peer influence is a real concern for almost every parent. Most parents remember all too well their own adolescent roller-coaster rides and understand the importance of peer groups as well as the need to fit in and have a sense of belonging. This need is especially strong for teenagers as they start the process of emancipating from their parents. They begin to push back during this process, and sometimes the pushing back lands them with a group of adolescents who look or act in ways that are problematic, negative, and destructive.

Maneuvering through adolescence has become more complicated in our society. For example, many families are led by overburdened single parents, drugs are widely available, and rapidly changing technology has changed the fabric of our children's social lives. Today's teens, and increasingly, younger children as well, have social Internet platforms (such as MySpace) and a broad spectrum of other potentially harmful Internet influences at their fingertips.

Mixed into the social and psychological factors shaping your child's behavior and belief system is *peer influence*. According to Jennifer Diebel, a psychotherapist who works with teens, your child may begin to act markedly different when he or she is being negatively influenced by his or her peer group. Like Trevor, your child may not seem like himself or herself. In other instances, negative peer influence may lead your child to become adept at deception, placating you at home but behaving badly away from home. Either way, parents need to be very tuned in and take steps to help their children avoid or distance themselves from negative peer groups.

FIRST STEPS

The first step in dealing with negative peer groups is prevention. If possible, steer your child away from negative peer groups before he or she becomes influenced by one. Even if your child is already involved with a negative peer group, the following steps may still be helpful.

+ Establish a strong family identity and sense of belonging.

We all need to know we belong somewhere. If children feel a strong sense of family identity, they will be less likely to look for belonging in negative places. For instance, the Jones family may be known for their Christian faith and committed involvement at their church, their love for the outdoors and camping, and their Sunday night feasts where guests are always welcome. The Jones children know this about their family, and it has filtered into their own individual identity. The Jones children also have a deep sense of belonging because their family identity is so strong. Both of these factors can help prevent negative peer involvement.

+ Help your child develop a strong sense of self.

Having a strong sense of self helps children stand firm in the face of negative peer pressure. Help your child discover what he or she does well. Encourage your child often with the reminder that God has uniquely designed him or her. Provide outlets for your child to explore interests and talents and affirm his or her individual strengths and needs.

+ Have ongoing family discussions about what type of friend constitutes a good friend and how to choose good friends.

Take a stroll down memory lane! Talk with your child about helpful friendships you had at his or her age. Then have an open discussion with your child about what he or she values in friendship. Be sure to revisit this topic as your child proceeds through school, as children develop and perceptions of friendship change. Discussions like this can guide a child's decisions about the type of people he or she chooses to hang out with. And if your child ends up in a negative peer situation, you can use this information to help him or her realize that the friendship isn't in his or her best interest.

NEXT STEPS

+ Redirect.

If you see evidence that your child is drifting toward a negative peer group, gently redirect him or her toward positive peer influences. Look for activities or groups that are compatible with your child's interests. If your child has always wanted to try a particular activity, this would be a perfect time! Consider a church youth group, drama club, art class, music, special interest group, enrichment program, youth travel experience, or any other social outlet that will capture your child's attention in a positive way.

+ Keep your child physically active.

Teenagers, especially boys, need a lot of outlets to burn off energy. In addition to providing a healthy, positive way for your child to spend his or her after-school time, sports activities can also provide a new group of peers. If your child resists team sports, try an individual sport or activity such as swimming, martial arts, an exercise or weight-lifting class, rock-climbing club, or skateboarding group.

+ Get your child involved in volunteering.

Helping others builds teenagers' confidence. If your child feels good about making a contribution to your community, he or she will be less attracted to negative peer groups and behavior. Many youth groups offer service projects or short-term mission trips. Teenagers and older-elementary kids may also enjoy serving younger kids by helping in Sunday school or volunteering at a local preschool or child care center.

+ Plan an exciting family trip.

An exciting family trip or an adventure camp can help distract your child from a negative peer group. Time away from the peer group in a new environment can help refocus your child and re-establish his or her independence. If your situation allows, you may even want to consider a special one-on-one trip with your child. Choose a destination that offers plenty of diversions that will interest you both.

+ Restrict your child from certain friendships.

If you have tried other alternatives but negative influences still persist, you may need to restrict your child from socializing with certain friends. Set aside a time when both parents are present to explain the unacceptable behaviors (of both your child and the negative peers) that led to the decision. Sincerely validate your child's feelings before moving on to establish boundaries and logical consequences for negative peer socialization.

+ Consider changing schools.

If negative peer influence is causing your child to behave in ways that endanger your child or others, you may want to remove your child from the negative peer group by changing schools. This is most effective if the negative peer group does not live in the surrounding neighborhood and if your child is not yet of driving age. Be prepared, though: Depending on your child's personality and how long he or she has attended the current school, your child may strongly protest this decision. Reserve this option for situations in which the potential for serious harm is great.

SCRIPTURE HELP

+ **1 Samuel 16:7**
+ **Proverbs 12:15**
+ **Proverbs 13:20**
+ **Proverbs 27:17**
+ **Romans 12:1-2**

+ **1 Corinthians 15:33**
+ **Ephesians 5:6-7**
+ **Ephesians 6:12-13**
+ **1 Timothy 4:12**
+ **2 Timothy 2:22**

Home Life

+ Make your home a safe haven.

Adolescents need a safe haven where they can just be themselves. Your child needs to know that you will love and accept him or her, no matter what. Providing that safe harbor at home helps your child want to be at home (instead of escaping to someplace else) when he or she is going through difficult situations.

+ Establish routine talk time.

Set aside a regular time when each family member has the opportunity to share what's going on in his or her life. Make a point of asking about work, school, and relationships. Many families choose to do this at mealtime, but it can be anytime that works for your family. Making this talk time a routine can strengthen your child's sense of family identity and belonging as well as build healthy patterns for family communication.

+ Model the behavior you would like to see in your child.

Make sure there is not a discrepancy between your behavior and the behavior you are requiring from your child. For instance, if you and your child are having a battle over bedtime or curfew time, make sure you model getting good rest as part of your lifestyle.

+ Don't react.

It's hard not to react emotionally when your child is negatively influenced by peers. However, the more you and your spouse can approach your child in a calm, unemotional manner, the more effective your communication will be. After thoughtful conversation with your spouse, ask your child to sit down with you for a conversation. Lay out your concerns, using specific examples. Ask for your child's input in solving the problem. Try to come up with a plan that you all agree with. Then make sure you stick to that plan and are consistent.

+ Give your child some private space.

Some parents begin snooping into their children's e-mails and journals before any real problem behavior has been demonstrated. They reason that it's better to be safe than sorry and that they're hoping to nip potential problems in the bud. While it's important to be proactive, snooping in your child's private communications will cause your child to distrust you and may make him or her feel as if there's no safe place at home to express private emotions and thoughts. Respecting your child's need for appropriate privacy helps establish trust and the feeling that home is a safe haven.

WHEN TO SEEK HELP

If you suspect your child is involved in a peer group that's involved with drugs, alcohol, or any other illegal behavior, act immediately.

Ask your child directly about his or her involvement. Make sure you're calm and have plenty of time for the conversation. Expect your child to deny the problem. Tell your child what you have seen, and let him or her know how you feel about it. Be specific about what you have observed and why it concerns you. Let your child know you'll be monitoring his or her activities more closely and that you'll be talking to other parents and school administrators about your observations. You might also meet with a mental health professional and/or school counselor to discuss your child's behavior and find additional resources to deal with it. Taking action as soon as you can on your child's behalf is vital.

What Not to Say

+ "You're ruining your life by hanging out with that group of kids."

As much as possible, avoid "you" statements. In addition, any words that shame your child can be very destructive. Keep your language focused on the behavior, not your child. Preface your statements with "I'm concerned that…" or "It worries me when you…because…"

+ "The kids you're hanging out with are bad kids."

Again, make sure your language does not focus on people as much as it does on the behaviors of people. Criticizing your child's friends, even when they're a negative influence, can cause your child to become more defensive and alienated.

+ "You can never hang out with those kids again."

Statements like this can send your child straight out the door. It's best if you help your child identify peers' negative behaviors for himself or herself. So before you forbid your child to socialize with certain peers, talk with your child about your concerns. Ask thought-provoking questions that will encourage your child to evaluate and judge peer relationships based on his or her defining values. For example, you might say, "How does [name] fit in with your other friends?" or "I've noticed that [name] is into [behavior of concern]. Is that really something you want to be around frequently?" By allowing your child to act on his or her own behalf, you'll strengthen your child's character. (However, if you know your child is engaging in dangerous behavior with these peers, you'll need to reserve the right to have the last word in this discussion.)

What to Say

+ "I can see why you want to be part of that group."

Affirming statements are very important. Jennifer Diebel tells parents to go by the 4 to 1 rule: For every one negative thing parents say, they need to say four positive things. Make it a habit to affirm the positive in your child as much and as frequently as you can. It may feel hard to affirm the negative peer group that is influencing your child. But if you look hard, you can probably find at least one positive reason for the association—your child chose these peers for a reason, after all. Keep in mind that affirmation can connect you with your child. It may also help minimize your child's defensiveness and create more room for you to communicate and find other ways to address the need the group is meeting for your child.

+ "Do you want to talk?"

Parents are the most important influence in a child's life. Even though it may appear that your adolescent is uninterested in your point of view, stay involved and don't stop trying to communicate with your child. Keep initiating conversations. Underneath your child's uninterested attitude is a deep need and a desire to be pursued and have regular positive parental input.

+ "I can totally understand how you feel."

Validating your child's feelings is very important. Validation helps build your parent-child relationship and also helps your child see that you aren't the enemy and you understand and empathize with him or her. If your child is willing to listen, you might also share how you experienced similar struggles at a similar age. (If you or your child is angry about a specific situation, your child may be more willing to hear this information later.)

ADDITIONAL RESOURCES

+ Books

Parenting Teens With Love and Logic. Foster Cline and Jim Fay. Colorado Springs, CO: Pinon Press, 2006.

Hurt: Inside the World of Today's Teens. Chap Clark. Grand Rapids, MI: Baker Academic, 2004.

+ Online Resources

www.crosswalk.com (a for-profit religious corporation dedicated to building up the church)

www.family.org/parenting (Focus on the Family's parenting site)

CHAPTER TWELVE

Pornography

Responding to a Child Who
Is Into Pornography

Luke is 13. When he was 10 years old, he accidentally found his dad's porn magazine in the garage. He has been seeing pornography on the computer since he was 11. Some of his friends send him picture e-mails on his cell phone and computer.

Sex is rarely discussed in Luke's home. His mom has said that sex is shameful and should be saved for marriage. Luke's parents don't show physical affection to each other in front of him. Once Luke walked into the kitchen and saw his parents kissing. They quickly stopped, acting guilty, when they realized he had entered the room.

Luke is insecure in his relationships with girls he finds attractive. He feels that if anyone really knew him, they would reject him because of his own feeling of badness. Due to his porn use, he is starting to view the girls in church and school as objects of sexual desire, and sometimes imagines their faces in the porn scenes he views. Luke knows that if the girls ever found out about his fantasies, they would probably never speak to him again, so he keeps his brief interactions focused on casual topics like schoolwork or the weather.

Luke's family doesn't talk about feelings. Only one person in the family is allowed to express anger: his dad. In order to escape the wrath of her husband, Luke's mom is usually passive in protecting her children. Luke knows he must hide his feelings to help keep the peace in the family.

Although he's intelligent, Luke doesn't excel in school. He's not praised at home when he does well. When his grades don't meet his parents' standards, however, he's harshly disciplined through words and rejection. Thus, he's afraid to trust his parents to meet his emotional needs. In fact, Luke feels he can't count on anyone to meet his needs.

When Luke is feeling bad, he always goes back to the same place: the websites that have allowed him to feel good before. After becoming aroused by looking at porn, he usually masturbates as he looks at the images. Luke feels shameful about his porn use. He thinks he's a bad person, that he must be the worst sinner among everyone he knows. As Luke continues to pull away from "less sinful people," he's becoming more isolated. The more isolated he becomes, the less likely it is that there will be an opportunity for someone to speak encouragement and grace into his life.

Luke knows that at least his websites will not reject him. As he looks, he fantasizes about the women and what they would do for him, both sexually and emotionally. Unfortunately, Luke finds that he is no longer excited by the first, "tamer" websites. He wants more and more explicit and arousing images. He begins to go to pornography as a reward when he experiences success in school or life. Luke spends more and more time looking at pornography on the Internet, sometimes hours at a time. This leads to even more shame and less emotional intimacy with others. Luke rationalizes that every guy does it, but he doesn't really know if this is true since he doesn't talk to anyone about it.

After school one day, his mom walked into his room while he was using porn. He was immediately embarrassed and ashamed before she said anything. Shocked and angry, she told him to turn off his computer immediately.

Not knowing what to do about this unplanned disclosure, she talked to her husband. Although he was more understanding of the temptation, he was upset and called Luke in for a discussion. Overwhelmed with shame, Luke confessed the frequency of his pornography use.

His parents called the pastor of their church for help. The pastor was familiar with Internet porn problems and suggested meeting with the family. In the meeting he suggested that Luke get help from a counselor who understands sex addiction and start meeting with the youth group, particularly with other guys his own age in a healthy environment. The pastor explained that this problem is based on the need for genuine, caring relationships with others. He explained to Luke's parents that they needed to start having weekly family meetings to share feelings and problems. He said that as scary as it is to know that Luke is into pornography, they must not condemn him but come beside him and help him work through relationships with friends and members of the family. Like everyone, Luke needs to be known, loved, and accepted for who God made him to be.

The family now meets with the pastor regularly and has agreed to be accountable for opening up to one another, to assess progress, and to work through additional issues as they arise.

Care and Counseling Tips

THE BASICS

Parents must be aware that pornography is very addictive. Porn appeals to people's deepest God-given need for intimacy. We live in a very sexualized culture in which sex sells everything from cereal to frozen pizza. Once kids get involved in online pornography, it can exercise enormous power over them.

Pornography is easy to find in our culture, even for kids. It's online, in magazines, books, videos, DVDs, and movies. Interest in pornography is progressive and grows in secrecy. According to XXXChurch.com, there are more than 300 million porn web pages, and 60 percent of all website visits are for sexual purposes. And now pornography is not just on computers but also on iPods and cell phones.

The average age that kids first see pornography is 11 years old, and some see it when they're even younger. And if you think this is an issue you have to worry about only with your son, think again. Thirty percent of people who look at pornography are female. This "dirty little secret" is stealing children's innocence: 80 percent of 15- to 17-year-olds who view pornography have had multiple hard-core exposures.

Because 87 percent of all teens are online, kids have plenty of opportunities to view pornographic websites. Americans between the ages of 13 and 18 spend more than 72 hours a week using electronic media, including the Internet, cell phones, television, music, and video games. And lest you think your younger child is immune, consider the fact that many comic or children's character names are linked to pornography sites. That means if your second-grader enters "Pokemon" or "Action Man" in a search engine, he or she may be a few innocent clicks away from an unwanted encounter with the darker side of the Internet. As many as 90 percent of 8- to 16-year-olds admit to having viewed pornography online, most while doing homework. And studies show that over half of kids in Christian schools have intentionally looked at pornography on the Internet.

Kids' reasons for viewing pornography can range from curiosity to addiction. In the most serious addictions, kids feel they can't live a day without it. As a parent, it's frightening to learn that a child can go from "just curious" to "can't live without it" in three days. That's how powerfully addictive pornography can be.

FIRST STEPS

+ Face reality.

Don't be naive about how easy it is for kids to access porn on the Internet. Over 40 percent of families say pornography is a problem in their homes. To access pornography, there is no need for a credit card; no passwords are required to get into many Internet sites. So-called free sites feature not just soft porn but also XXX videos.

+ Build relationships.

Be a positive resource by building a secure attachment with your child. Children learn the skills required to maintain intimate relationships from their parents, for good or ill. Your child is much less likely to turn to pornography if his or her need for a loving, communicative relationship is met in your home.

Your child needs to be in healthy same-sex relationships through such groups as a youth group, scouts, and sports teams. Bless the uniqueness of your child with others who have similar interests. Help your child explore new interests.

+ Start building a positive, healthy, biblical view of sexuality when your children are young.

Take time to answer your child's questions about sexuality and his or her body. Don't put the conversation off until you think your child is "old enough." Adolescence has enough awkward moments without adding a first conversation about sexuality, and by this time many Internet-savvy kids will have already found the information on their own. Teach your child that sex is natural—in fact, it is God-given. Explain to your child that sex is good, healthy, and a beautiful gift in the context of marriage.

SCRIPTURE HELP

+ **Genesis 2:18-25**
+ **Matthew 5:28**
+ **Mark 7:14-21**
+ **Romans 13:12-14**

+ **1 Corinthians 6:12-20**
+ **Galatians 5:16-25**
+ **Ephesians 5:1-5**
+ **1 Thessalonians 4:3-7**

+ Know the warning signs.

Unusual behavior or demonstrations of guilt or shame may be cause for concern. Viewing your child's Internet browsing history may turn up porn links. However, depending on the level of addiction, some kids may be smart enough to clear the history after using the computer. If your child's browsing history is frequently blank, you may want to gently ask, "What are some websites you've looked at recently?" At first, your child may lie or deny he or she has looked at porn sites. In this case, you'll need to lovingly reassure your child that you are concerned about his or her behavior and want to help, not condemn, him or her.

Risk factors for developing a dependency on pornography include past or current abuse, a disengaged and rigid family system, and negative messages about sexuality. If you suspect that pornography may be a problem for your child, tread gently. By making a big deal of your child's exploration of or interest in pornography, you may intimidate him or her.

When it comes to relationships, we're all insecure! Above all, be honest (at a level appropriate for your child's age) with your child about your own struggles. When parents are honest, children are likely to listen and talk openly about sexual issues.

NEXT STEPS

+ Revisit the sex talk.

Talk about physical development and arousal, how babies are conceived, the sexual response cycle, birth control, STDs, and the risks of premarital sex. Be open to talking about sexual matters often so sex is not shrouded in secrecy. As much as possible, set aside your inhibitions and talk openly with your child about the arousal he or she is experiencing through pornography. Point out that, although powerful, sexual attraction is only a part of a healthy, long-lasting relationship. Pornographic images are not healthy examples of real relationships between real people with real needs. Teach your child about healthy give and take within relationships.

+ Be physical.

It's critical that you demonstrate your love for your child through physical affection. Modest physical affection between parents is also important because it shows your child that sexuality is meant to be part of a healthy marriage. Even if you're a single parent, you can still send positive messages about sexuality. Affirm your child's gender, appearance, qualities, and abilities. Talk about your son's masculinity or your daughter's femininity. Build your child's self-esteem through healthy, loving relationships.

+ Develop a method for talking about sex and pornography.

Take your child on a special date or overnight trip to talk about this important subject one on one. If you feel uncomfortable bringing up the subject, try reading an age-appropriate book on the subject together. (*God's Design for Sex,* by Stan and Brenna Jones, is a series of books designed for just this purpose and includes separate volumes for ages 3 to 5, 5 to 8, 8 to 11, and 11 to 14.) If your child is into pornography, he or she may claim to already "know it all." Use this time to create a genuine dialogue with your child. Listen earnestly to what he or she knows, and be prepared to amend misinformation. Stress that the sexual acts on the Internet do not represent real relationships. Even though your child may have amassed sexual knowledge beyond his or her years, he or she has probably lost or bypassed the understanding of true emotional intimacy. Use this conversation to re-establish for your child that sexual attraction is a means of achieving intimacy, not (as it is often depicted in the media) an end in itself.

Be honest with your child about your own sexual brokenness and struggles you may have experienced in relationships. Remind your child that God can help him or her break the addiction to pornography and restore a right attitude about relationships. Close your time together by thanking God for the gift of your child's sexuality.

+ Get help from pastors and counselors who understand sex addiction.

You may require specialized help to get to the core of the need your child has tried to satisfy by viewing pornography. It's not enough to stop the unwanted activity; you must identify the reason your child is drawn to pornography and has kept going back to it.

+ Guide your child into healthy relationships.

Your child needs to know that he or she is accepted by peers. Real relationships with real people do cause stress, but they also offer the opportunity to be loved. The need for love and acceptance is universal, and it is this unsatisfied need that often drives people to pornography. Humans may be broken in relationships, but we are also healed in relationships. Help your child explore interests and activities that lead him or her to meet others in healthy arenas. Offer guidance when those relationships cause pain, helping your child learn and grow through them.

WHEN TO SEEK HELP

If your child is addicted to pornography, he or she will probably need help to break this powerful addiction. Seek professional help from pastors or counselors who have experience with sex addiction when you suspect pornography use and your child

+ **spends too much time on the computer,**
+ **neglects important things or people in his or her life, or**
+ **becomes secretive about his or her web usage.**

Home Life

+ Create conversations around the media.

Sex is everywhere in our culture. Instead of avoiding the subject by turning off the TV, mute the TV and talk about the messages it's sending. Ask
your child age-appropriate questions to determine how much of the message he or she has taken in. For older kids and teens, challenge your child
to compare the media's messages about sexuality with the messages he or
she has received at home or in church.

+ Protect your child from exposure to pornography.

If you believe your child may be addicted to pornography, get ready to
clean house! Get rid of any adult pornography, including magazines and
PG-13 or R-rated movies that feature sex scenes or other highly suggestive
material. Cancel your cable TV, or use parental controls to block inappropriate stations.

   Relocate your family computer to a more public place in your home. In
addition, consider using a computer filter (although some computer-savvy
teens may figure out ways to bypass this). Accountability programs are also
available that allow you to track where on the Internet your child has been.
Be sure to teach your child how to handle Internet privacy issues—when
asked, 14 percent of 7- to 17-year-olds said they would give out an e-mail
address, and 29 percent would give a street address.

+ Make home a place to share feelings.

Make the intimacy of sharing feelings an ongoing daily ritual and guiding force in your home. Designate mealtimes or other family times as
"safe sharing" times. When family time is neglected, addictions can take
root. As your child grows, help him or her discover that even awkward or
uncomfortable feelings can be handled with God's help.

What Not to Say

+ "Sex is dirty."
Sex is God's design for intimacy. Pornography is a perversion of sex. If your child develops a negative view of sex now, he or she may encounter problems in relationships or marriage as an adult. Instead, say something like "Sex is special" or "Sex is an expression of love."

+ "You should be ashamed."
Curiosity is a natural part of sexuality. Talk with your child about why he or she was curious about those particular websites. Answer any questions, and help your child understand his or her own feelings.

+ "Just give it to God."
While your child may know this cognitively, he or she may feel very far from God during this stressful time. Rather than urging your child to trust God more, talk honestly with your child about his or her feelings and fears. Pray for or with your child about these things.

What to Say

+ "Sex is God's idea and is a beautiful gift."
Talk, talk, and talk some more. Demonstrate God's gift of physical affection by hugging your child. Kiss your spouse when he or she enters and leaves the house (and any other time you feel like it). Affirm your child's curiosity and the masculinity or femininity that God gave him or her.

+ "What do you need?"
Help your child understand his or her own feelings. If your child has turned to pornography, he or she probably has a deep need for acceptance that is not being met. Your child may be lonely or may need more or deeper con-

nections with real people. It's also possible that your child has been hurt or abused in some way. If this is the case, you should seek professional help as you support your child. Sometimes children may just need more of your time. In our busy world, it's often hard to stop and just listen.

ADDITIONAL RESOURCES

+ Books

Wild at Heart: Discovering the Secret of a Man's Soul. John Eldredge. Nashville, TN: Thomas Nelson, 2006.

Breaking Free: Understanding Sexual Addiction & the Healing Power of Jesus. Russell Willingham. Downers Grove, IL: InterVarsity Press, 1999.

In the Shadow of the Net: Breaking Free of Compulsive Online Sexual Behavior. Patrick Carnes, David Delmonico, Elizabeth Griffen. Center City, MN: Hazelden Publishing & Educational Services, 2004.

Craving for Ecstasy: How Our Passions Become Addictions and What We Can Do About Them. Harvey Milkman, Stanley Sunderwirth. San Francisco, CA: Jossey-Bass Publishers, 1998.

How and When to Tell Your Kids About Sex: A Lifelong Approach to Shaping Your Child's Sexual Character. Stan and Brenna Jones. Colorado Springs, CO: NavPress, 2007.

+ Online Resources

http://.XXXChurch.com (an online parachurch ministry dedicated to providing hope and healing for those affected by pornography)

www.family.org/protection/#safety (Focus on the Family)

www.internetsafety.com/safe-eyes (provides Internet safety solutions)

www.x3watch.com/index.php (accountability software designed to help with online integrity)